Sophia Associates

*E*veryDay Epiphanies is a collection of essays based on Ms. Rodriguez's online newsletter by the same name. Over the course of many years of writing, and inspired by her experience coaching hundreds of individuals, Ms. Rodriguez has compiled powerful questions and practical suggestions to life's ordinary challenges. Her insight into the sacredness of our lives allows the reader to glimpse the extraordinary in the ordinary. Through her own personal experiences and profound conversations with her clients Ms. Rodriguez explores the soul and its role in how we think, feel and behave. Woven throughout the book readers will find practices and exercises for living with purpose and on purpose.

This is a book that can be picked up at any time and enjoyed by turning to the essay that moves the reader in the moment. Ms. Rodriguez's humor combined with her passion for what it means to be human shines through in simple language even as she grapples with life's complexities. As advisor, witness and wisdom partner, she takes you through a journey shared by all of us.

EveryDay Epiphanies

Insights for Living with Purpose

EveryDay Epiphanies
copyright 2007 Alicia Rodriguez

Published by Sophia Associates, Inc.

Layout and Cover Design
by Blooming Twig Books LLC.
www.bloomingtwigbooks.com

First Edition 2007.

ISBN 978-0-9797958-0-0

Dedication

Dedicated to my son Joseph
who inspires me to notice the extraordinary
moments of my ordinary life
and to my husband Gerard
whose partnership in my life's journey
has defined unconditional love
and true friendship.

Table of Contents

Chapter Three:
Beliefs and Reflections   **088**

Chapter Four: Work and Goals   **124**

EveryDay Epiphanies

Insights for Living with Purpose

Introduction

Epiphany: a moment of sudden revelation or insight

*A*lmost everyone I know has experienced an "epiphany" at some time in their lives. These sudden insights can shift how we experience our lives sustaining us through difficult times or even changing the course of our lives.

One of the most powerful epiphanies that I have ever experienced came from a very simple, ordinary event. I had been walking by the Severn River, near where I was living, with Joseph, my (at the time) three-year old son. He had paused to look at what I thought was a flower, and was almost nose-to-nose with it. I walked over to see what had made him so curious about this flower. He said to me, "Mommy, this is the most beautiful flower I have ever seen. And look Mommy, the flower has wings."

Joseph was seeing a butterfly for the very first time and unbelievably, the beautiful creature was content to sit quietly as it was admired. He whispered, "Mommy, look at the lines and colors!" As I carefully leaned in to take a closer look, the true beauty of the butterfly was revealed to me. I could see the delicate texture of the wings, the colorful spots that reflected the sunshine, the fine legs rooting it to the leaf. And I thought, I have never really *seen* a butterfly! I have looked at many butterflies but always as they flitted by. It was only because of the stillness of the moment, the quiet joy of walking by the water and my attention to Nature and to my son, that a door opened, allowing me to see something extraordinary even in this butterfly sighting, which I would have customarily considered an ordinary, every day event.

This book is about pausing to notice the extraordinary in our ordinary lives. It is about those epiphanies that we miss when we don't slow down long enough to really pay attention. And we miss so many!

Our lives often move with such high velocity that life begins to look like a blur; spending most of our energy in just keeping up with survival. We miss the moments that make up our days and suddenly we "wake up" and we might be fifty years old and still on the treadmill wondering where it all went and 'For goodness sake, why am I still doing this'? We have forgotten in our haste the time when we could savor the moment, when we actually tasted the sweetness of a summer strawberry, the chill of a chocolate sundae and the joy of cuddling in bed amidst warm blankets on a winter morning.

What are you missing? Do you want to retrieve the moments that fly by? I want this for you and for myself. That is why I wrote *EveryDay Epiphanies*. Because maybe by sharing my epiphanies and those of some friends, you too may slow down long enough to notice the simple, every day moments that allow your epiphanies to surface.

You can read this book cover to cover, or like a leisurely stroll, you can pick and choose where you want to begin, and where you want to end at any given time. Keep it by your nightstand and start your morning by reading one entry, and as you go through your day, pay attention and focus on what you discovered in reading that entry. Perhaps end your day reading a passage, and as you drift to sleep, an insight, an epiphany emerges, morphing into a powerful dream. Sit under a tree with a picnic and stroll through the pages while you feel the sun and breeze and pause to contemplate how a passage may reflect something in your life.

Share this book with someone you care about. Give them the gift of opening up to a page that opens a door to their own epiphany. They may re-connect to their essential self, bringing them to an inspired decision to live in harmony with what brings them joy and a sense of purpose and meaning. They too may notice something truly extraordinary in something as ordinary as a butterfly.

The sight of a monarch butterfly will always take me back to that moment by the water with my son. And as long as it does, I will remember that being attentive to life, savoring moment by moment, is the key to my own personal enlightenment. It will always remind me to slow down, be present, and enjoy my life wherever I am and whatever I am doing. And I will smile as I stroll through my journey. I hope you do too.

Blessings,

Alicia
September, 2007
Annapolis, MD

Chapter One
Self and Spirit

"I hope you go out and let stories happen to you, and that you will work them, water them with your blood and tears and your laughter till they bloom, till you yourself burst into bloom."
~Clarissa Pinkola Estes

Stories and Poetry

June 15, 2002 - 11:30 p.m.

OK, it's late. All I can think about is sinking my toes into grainy sand on "our" island in Maine. But not yet. I am still in my office writing at 11:30 p.m. I promised myself I would go to bed. But here I am – why?

When I used to write with pen and paper (yes, I am that old!) I used to say that my pen had taken a walk. A voice in my head would utter the words and I would take dictation. That is how I would write. Usually, there would be something behind the voice, an experience, a word, an image that would be so compelling that it would pour out of the pen like gooey liquid, filling the spaces between the lines. Only in the quiet could I hear the voice speak and only then would I grab something, a newspaper, a napkin, lipstick, anything that I could write with. It would be compelling – and fleeting.

I have that sensation now, right now. I cannot sleep until I finish here. There is something that needs to be expressed. Not like an answer, more like a question or an observation.

In 1992 I wrote, "It's amazing how much I learn from helping someone else sort out their difficulties. It's like my own light bulbs go on…what I call the "AHA" way of learning. Their discovery becomes mine as well. Life is full of these little, major discoveries sun breaks of clarity usually brought on by clouds of confusion."

For every conversation I have, there is a point in which I shift. There is openness, a paying attention to what the language expresses, even as the underlying may be inexpressible. A combination of intuition and pragmatism asserts itself. What would it be like if all of us would be open to our own intuition, not to the exclusion of the pragmatic, but more as an adjunct to it? How would our decisions be different? Why do we seek to justify with data when our hearts tell us the truth? Can a heart lie? I suppose it depends on the heart's ability to express and the individual's openness to listen. I don't know.

As distinct as the individuals I coach, so appear the conversations. But stop, look beyond the words, and I find similarities, the basis for our humanity. There are stories, so many stories. There are emotions, so many emotions. There is poetry in each individual. Discovery, acceptance, forgiveness, right action, brazenness, courage, love, disappointment, compassion, everything!

I am blessed. I know that. I am privileged to share in the lives of others and be witness to the breaking open of so many cocoons. I must acknowledge – and thank – all who have contributed to the experience of my life.

So perhaps between lines of poetry and the subtle sounds of the "AHA" moments, there is a coalescence of what it is to be human. And here I am, witness to that, needing to thank you for allowing me to be in the space between the clouds of confusion and the sun breaks of clarity.

You will read this and I will be on that island in Maine, listening to the harsh breaking of the waves on rocks carved by a lifetime of power. I will be sitting atop one of those large rocks overlooking the ocean, spray in my face and only the cries of the gulls to interfere with my thoughts.

Waking Up to the Question: Who Am I?

*T*he moon was full the evening before my Dad died. I was in Maine at school walking back in the wee hours after an all night party. The air tasted of wet pine and my LL Bean boots sloshed through the melting snow pooling after an early morning shower. It was May but the winter overstays its welcome in Maine.

I don't remember ever seeing a moon like the one that evening. The light from the moon was bright enough to guide me back to the dorm. It was quiet and still. I felt safe.

Maybe it was the drinks, the freedom of dancing all night or the feeling of being incubated from the world. I could throw the question to the icy stillness, the one I didn't know how to answer as I approached graduation day, and expect an answer to whisper back.

Who am I? I wondered. I had completed four years of school, lived in Europe, and with a sense of adventure born of youth, hitchhiked and backpacked, staying at homes when strangers took us in. I thought I knew who I was when I started but this new person, I didn't quite know her. Who am I...becoming? I was still becoming her with only an inkling of what lay ahead.

The ringing phone rudely awakened me with news that I must return home. My head pounding I packed a bag and sped home in a borrowed car I demanded exceed all speed limits. The news of his death stunned me.

I was different from that moment on. The answer changed suddenly and dramatically. No whispers, just a loud scream beckoning me to take care of my family. That is who I became – caretaker.

The year my Dad died, 1976, is the first time I remember asking myself this fundamental question. Who am I? Several times in my life I thought I knew the answer only to find out that I was carrying an old way of being into a totally new way of life. Usually, I come to ask myself this question when I am uncertain, or when my life is shifting from one way to another way of living but I haven't quite caught up. If I am really paying attention, I can hear the whisper coming from my soul, telling me whether I am who I say I am or if I am living someone else's life.

I now know to ask the answer often. I now know that the moment the answer leaves my lips, I begin to morph into a new answer. Each answer is a moment in time, infinite moments projecting how the essential self chooses to manifest. That question is the foundation for living on purpose. I must ask it often, throwing the question to the stillness so it can return powerfully, calibrating the course of my life to align with the deepest part of who I am, at the level of my soul.

Is it time for you to ask yourself the question: Who am I? Are you really happy right now in your life? Are you uncomfortable, intuitively knowing that a shift is occurring but not taking steps to intentionally bring the whole of who you are, right now, into action to support a positive shift?

Here is what I have learned about inviting the question and listening for the true answer.

1. **Stillness.** Consciously create still (mental, emotional, physical, spiritual) space in your life. If you cannot meditate, go for quiet walks in Nature. Leave the "to do" list at home. Take a break at work, far from the electronics and chatter.

2. **Get Back to the Earth.** If you like to garden, get

your hands into the dirt, hug a tree, watch your vegetables grow and bring nourishment to your table. If you like animals, go play with them, watch them, listen to them.

3. Friendships. Surround yourself with loving people who value you for who you are, just the way you are; individuals who tell the truth and manifest personal integrity; friends who energize you and challenge you to be the very best *you*.

4. Spiritual Practice. Explore your own spirituality, be it in the form of a structured religion, or prayer before your own personal altar. Connect with the Divine, however you conceive this to be.

5. Take Care of Yourself. You need to honor and nourish your body, heart and mind. When you feel healthy and well rested you are better able to remain centered in the answer to your question, even in the face of resistance and challenges.

6. 48 Hours to Live. Imagine that you only had 48 hours to live. What would you do? Who would you be with? Where would you be? The answers to these questions will point to those values you hold dearest.

7. Who Am I? This is a koan (a riddle that cannot be unraveled with the mind) that the Zen Masters ask of their pupils. And ask, and ask, and ask. Use the koan; ask yourself this question at least 50 times (really!). Write down the answers…listen; here is an opportunity to hear your Soul Voice!

8. Ask Others Whom You Trust. Sometimes we cannot see ourselves clearly and need to ask others about how we are special. Allow them to give you the gift of reflection.

9. Apply These Questions to Your Work or Business. Has your business environment been changing since the time you put out your shingle or were hired for the position you are now in? How does your personal evolution impact shifts that may be occurring in your work and vice versa?

10. Letting Go. Many times we deny our soul voice because it means letting go of things of the past, or past behaviors or beliefs. We cling to them for dear life, preferring the known to the unknown. If you are asking yourself, "Who Am I?" for the first time in years, you may discover a different answer that will require new strategies, perhaps a transformation of your beliefs.

Thirty years later, I still find myself asking the question: Who Am I? Each time I answer it I discover new ways of being in the world, different aspects of myself and countless creative expressions of who I am. It is a wonderful journey. I hope you discover your own answer in the stillness. It is worth the asking.

"It is only with my eyes closed that I can see."
~ Alicia Rodriguez

To See With Eyes Closed

One of my reflective practices is to walk the labyrinth. I usually ask for guidance or clarification on some issue. One day, I just wanted to be present to whatever occurred.

As I wound my way around the labyrinth, following the circuitous path, I could hear all kinds of chatter in my head. I was hearing reminders of things I had yet to do, unfinished thoughts that were demanding attention, problems that I had not yet resolved and mundane observations that really didn't mean much. It all sounded like static.

Eventually the rhythm of my walking calmed the noise so by the time I reached the center, it was quieter inside me. This is where I tend to pause for a while, to return to my inner center. I closed my eyes as I stood in the center, the sun shining down on me. And I heard what I had not been able to hear through the static in my mind.

I heard the cardinals in the trees. I heard the flow of the water from the river below. I felt the wind on my skin and heard it rustling the new leaves on the trees. I heard the echo of voices somewhere from the dock on the river. I could feel the warmth of the sun on my face and noticed that I was thirsty. And then I heard my own inner voice observe: "It is only with my eyes closed that I can see."

Like a mantra, this statement kept repeating as I walked around and out of the labyrinth. What did it mean?

Since then I have noticed that when I think I know something, I impose that "knowledge" on the situation but it keeps me from noticing what might actually be there. I enter into the situation already full of what I believe and it keeps me from being open and present to what is possible or what is there.

I get uncomfortable when I don't know the answer. When I began to notice this, I began to make a shift. At one coaching session I could feel myself wanting to "solve" my client's issue, to give him the solution. And I could see how that was keeping me from being completely present to him, even in his confusion. Once I allowed myself to be with him and his confusion, and my not knowing, my senses kicked in where my mind had been. My mind had been trying to solve a problem and it had blocked what was right there in the room. But by moving into "sensing" I was able to observe and to state what I was observing and sensing. And it was from that place of sensing without knowing that a breakthrough occurred.

Indeed, I had to "close my eyes so I could see". I had to enter into the dark not-knowing place and trust my feelings and intuition. And I had to be still inside of myself to do this. I had to quiet my own chatter in order to remain present. I came to understand that my mind is a powerful tool. But that it can also be the path of least resistance - the comfortable way of being-that I default to. And if that is so, then it may block other ways of knowing that come from a less comfortable place.

So here is what I want to leave you with. What parts of you are you using consistently that have worked well for you in your life? Notice if you are using that as a default because it is known, because it is a comfortable way of being or a way of doing things that makes it easier for you. Ask yourself, if it isn't time to open yourself to some discomfort and learn to enlist other aspects of yourself.

If you tend to live in your mind, how could you use your body to learn? Or if you tend to be highly analytical, how can you exercise the muscle of intuition? How can you use all the gifts and talents you have available to you; not only the ones you are used to using? And what can you do on a regular basis to find the stillness that allows you to really hear and see and be present? What does your inner center feel like and how can this be a source of knowing for you? If you don't know, or if you have forgotten, perhaps it is time to reconnect to a greater wisdom.

Be still. Listen. Close your eyes. And see.

To Be the Person You Are

*I*f you write, you know what it fees like to start with a blank sheet. The white void can either frighten or invite me. When frightened by this looming void I search for inspiration in poetry, books and people. I picked up a favorite inspirational book and opened to the quote above, knowing that wherever I opened up, that would be the place I would write about.

I love the way the quote starts. "It is easy to be the person you have always been…" At least, it certainly appears easy to be easy to be yourself. What I do know from coaching is you often want to be anyone but yourself. It isn't that easy to be exactly who you are, authentically, when the world imposes all its "shoulds" on you. You can expend huge amounts of energy in your upkeep of who you have been. And in the meantime, you have ignored or simply not become aware of who you are becoming.

Sometimes suddenly, sometimes slowly, your unhappiness and discomfort begins to assert itself to the point where you no longer tolerate the feeling that you are not living according to what matters most to you. You realize that you are paying a price for living someone else's version of your life.

"It requires no change, no self-reflection, no growth…" Habits create complacency. You allow yourself to become numb, trading potential for ease. Others tell you that you should be afraid of reaching outside of your current situation in life. With best intentions they quickly caution you about failing, revealing their own self-doubts and limitations. Why, you might even succeed and then what? You may become the person you are, doing what you were meant to do in this lifetime!

"It may appear that changing yourself requires giving up something…" In a deck of tarot cards, the most feared card is the Death card. That is what transitions may feel like to you. Stepping out of your nice, comfy zone feels like giving something up, something that you dare not let go of. It may feel as if a part of your being is dying. But indeed, the transition, like the Death card, is a representation of a change, of an evolution, and, if done with right intentions, you come home to your essential self.

"In reality, there is no need to give up anything – you simply add to what has been." You tend to polarize your situation seeing possibilities as mutually exclusive instead of searching how you might creatively include multiple aspects of your desired life. You cannot eliminate your experiences. You can transform how you perceive your experiences in ways that fuel your next evolution.

To be the person you are is to expand and retreat at the same time. In your external world you expand who you are by adding new dimensions to your life. In your internal world, you retreat to the beginning, to the essential Self, that dearly wants and needs to be acknowledged and represented, perhaps in new ways that may at first be surprising.

To be fully the person you are is the only thing your soul demands. You will pay a price for living someone else's life, when living our own, big, perfect, beautiful life was all that you are meant to do.

"To be nobody — but yourself — in a world which is
doing its best, night and day, to make you everybody
else — means to fight the hardest battle
which any human being can fight,
and never stop fighting.
~e.e. cummings

Crossing Boundaries: Too Far to Go

N ow he has really gone too far", she said on the phone. "Not only have I gone way beyond what I said I would do, but I haven't even asked for any thing in return. How could he take advantage of me like that?" My answer was: "He hasn't."

Normally, one would think I would be more empathetic, but this was a person with a pattern of allowing others to go too far beyond her "boundaries". She had not yet defined and articulated what these boundaries were, only sensing frustration and resentment when she intuitively felt imposed upon.

What is a boundary? Is it territory you claim as your own? Is it a wall you construct to keep others out? Is it solid, or permeable? How is a boundary set? Webster's online dictionary defines boundary as: a line or plane indicating the limit or extent of something, a line determining the limits of an area. Let's consider and reframe these definitions in light of being human.

First, the boundary can be defined as a personal demarcation of held values that maintains wholeness and integrity. By that same definition, a boundary is a personal tool that keeps you whole, distinct, alive, supported and healthy. It is based on values you hold to be essential to your well-being and happiness. These values could be: time with family, education, hobbies, honesty, work ethic, service and more.

Crossing a boundary can diminish or compromise your wholeness. If you understand what matters to you then a boundary can be more easily defined and articulated.

The definition of boundary includes a limit. A limit differentiates me from you, self from other. It too maintains wholeness and integrity and sense of individuality. You can state, without apology or judgment, who you are and what you need that may be different than who others are and what others need.

Confronted with a difficult decision, you can choose wisely when you have defined and articulated your boundaries. Others don't cross your boundaries; you allow them to cross your boundaries. How can you set boundaries that support your well-being, goals, dreams and happiness?

• **Get to know yourself.** Who you are will determine what elements of life make you happy. These elements will be distinctly yours – not someone else's.

• **Tell others.** You have to "train" those around you to respect your boundaries by articulating what you value and what is acceptable or not acceptable to you.

• **Know that you can choose.** Making decisions will be easier when you are sure of what is not acceptable. You will begin to choose for yourself, no longer allowing someone else to orchestrate your life.

• **Understand that boundaries are permeable.** Boundaries act as filters; they keep out the nasty stuff and allow the good stuff to come through. They are not solid walls that keep out relationships, love and friendship. Instead, these permeable boundaries affirm great relationships, love and friendship!

• **Relationships are improved by boundaries.** Imagine that your partner and those around you understand what your boundaries are and what his/her own boundaries are. Out of commitment or friendship he/she could articulate when boundaries are being crossed and perhaps be able to resolve issues before they become large-scale conflicts and misunderstandings.

• **Respect is one by-product of boundaries.** Authenticity and self-acceptance are others. What keeps you from setting, articulating or maintaining your boundaries?

• **"I don't know what matters to me."** If you don't know what matters to you chances are you won't know what makes you happy and maintains your personal wholeness.

• **"But they won't want/love/care/respect me anymore!"** Although one of the greatest fears associated with setting and maintaining your boundaries has to do with the fear of loss of a relationship, doing so gently, lovingly and honestly will either improve a healthy relationship or it will eliminate a draining relationship. If the relationship is based on genuine caring and respect, articulating your boundaries will be an exercise that draws you closer.

• **"But I will lose my job, spouse, career, etc."** Again, the greatest fear around claiming your boundaries has to do with loss. How long are you willing to be in a job that you hate or work in an organization whose culture squeezes the life from you? How long can you remain in an abusive or unloving relationship that diminishes you constantly? Have you actually examined your career to determine if it is aligned with what matters to you? If these are the things you fear losing, perhaps now is the time to re-evaluate what really matters to you so you can begin a life of wholeness and happiness.

• **"Life is compromise."** Sorry, I just won't accept that. There is a distinction between compromise and accommodation. Compromising takes from you, from who you are authentically and what you value. You give up something in order to get something less than what you want or deserve. This leaves you feeling disempowered and unhappy. To accommodate is a temporary situation where you consciously choose to adjust a boundary for something else that for the moment may be more important. You are empowering yourself to make a conscious decision that has an outcome you desire. Stress results from compromising. Ask where, when and how much are you either compromising or accommodating? And is that what you really want to do?

• **An unspoken belief that others are more important than you are.** Many women, in particular, have been brought up to nurture others first. When trying to assert your boundaries you may be called selfish yet indeed it is an attitude of self-care that allows you to truly nurture those that you care about and model a healthy lifestyle.

• **Saying no to one thing is saying yes to another and vice versa.** You may have difficulty saying, "no" to others, (which is a word that really means "yes" to yourself). Next time this happens, try saying, "Let me get back to you" or "Let me think about that". This practice trains you to consciously choose whether or not to comply and it provides the space for you to choose on purpose. Soon, you will find yourself saying no because you understand that you are as important as others. You will discover that getting your needs met is not exclusive of meeting the needs of others or handling your responsibilities. The word "selfish" simply means self-care. It does not mean "at the expense of others." Often we perceive our self-care to be in opposition of caring for others. Remember, in an airplane when oxygen masks fall in emergencies, the instruction is to place your mask on first, then your child's. Why do you think that is?

• **"It's just not worth the pain and conflict."** Most people do not enjoy conflict and will go to any lengths to avoid conflict. I can only suggest that there is a price to pay in silencing oneself. Resentment is one of the best indicators that you are not setting good boundaries. Consider that entering into conflict with honesty and compassion may bring about a breakthrough in your relationships and elsewhere.

When you commit to live your life aligned with what matters most to you amazing possibilities arise. Setting boundaries for yourself will be easier. You will attract relationships based on respect and care and you will enjoy renewed energy at work. The whining will cease and in its place you may hear a resounding roar full of vitality and joy!

"Throughout the history of mankind there have been murderers and tyrants; and while it may seem momentarily that they have the upper hand, they have always fallen. Always."
~Mahatma Gandhi

Getting Your Needs Met

How many times have you begun a conversation in anger or desperation with, "But I need you to do this..." or "I need this or that." By the time you articulate your needs, the threshold has been crossed and the statement may come across as a weak whimper.

Everyone has needs. Some needs are fundamental, such as the need to be loved or to be appreciated. If you are aware of the role your needs play in your decisions and your behaviors, you can fulfill your needs before they become overwhelming or result in huge conflict. Meeting your needs is the precursor to getting what you want. If you want something, first be sure that your needs are not getting in the way of achieving your goals.

Here are some ways to get your needs met:

• Decide what you need, what is essential for you to thrive and be happy.

• Once you recognize which needs are not being fulfilled, purposely create opportunities to get your needs met.

• State the need to another person so that the person is aware that this need is present. This is especially true in relationships. For example, one client complained that her husband never asked about her day; he entered the house immediately talking about his day and after "venting" and feeling better, he read the paper. But he never asked about her day. We decided that she would make a direct request to her husband to inquire about her day upon arriving home. As a result of asking her about her day first, she was better able to listen to and empathize with him. Her attention no longer was with her unmet need; her attention was focused on her husband. Curiously, his response to her request was that he had not realized that she felt this way because she was always so upbeat. He didn't even realize that this was an issue until she spoke of it. Lesson: asking others for support will help them relate better and minimize your unmet needs.

• Create a bookends situation where you put yourself in a position to get your need met, and then ask for feedback about that. For example, if you are finding a lack of challenging projects at work, volunteer for projects that would challenge you and provide learning and success. You create the opening to get your need for achievement met, and you then validate and celebrate your achievement.

• Create structures that support your needs. If you decide to focus on taking better care of yourself, one option might be to free up time to leverage opportunities to exercise, or to spend time with your family and friends.

Ultimately, you are responsible for getting your needs met. Don't depend on others to know what these are. Make direct, specific requests, find alternatives and create structures in your life that position you to have your needs met. When you act on purpose you open the way for more flow in your life and better connection to others.

"No one knows what makes the soul wake up so happy!
Maybe a dawn breeze has blown the veil from the face of God."
~Jelaluddin Rumi

The Power of Pause

We are a society where more means better and speed is an enhancement. There is no space in our lives to "pause", to reflect, and to gain perspective when there is so much to be done. You are evaluated on results that reflect a cultural bias for velocity. When you want to achieve something, your natural inclination is to take action. And there are many times that this is exactly what is called for. However, when taking action becomes a knee-jerk reaction to everything, it becomes a pattern of behavior that arises from non-thinking. How much more powerful would your actions be if they were preceded by a pause, however small, to reflect on the appropriate action to take, or the right words to use to communicate, or to create a space to defuse a volatile situation?

May I suggest using P-A-U-S-E in your future encounters to see how you may feel less stressed, more confident and better prepared to meet the demands placed on you. Here is what I mean by "PAUSE".

P – **is for Patience**. Be patient with the situation or with the people around you or even with yourself. Patience takes practice. Being patient does not mean being soft, indecisive or slow. It is more like surrendering to a situation that you cannot control. And in surrendering, you can accept the situation, see it more clearly and deal with it more appropriately.

A – **is for Allow**. Allow yourself some space to think in any given situation. For example, one of the challenges all of us face in our environments is interruptions and demands on our time and resources. Instead of brushing off a co-worker abruptly because he/she is interrupting you, acknowledge them, tell them that in order to really address their concerns you need to finish what you are doing and tell them when you will get back to them with an answer or time to speak. Your co-worker will leave feeling heard, you will be able to finish your task and you will not feel the stress of being rushed into a conversation or decision while leaving something else incomplete.

U – is for Understand. Stephen Covey has a saying: "Seek first to understand, then be understood." In order to respond to another person, you have to first LISTEN. You cannot listen when you are rushed or when your mind is chattering away. "PAUSE" gives you the space to quiet your mind in a way that allows you to really listen so that you can frame your communication so it can be received and heard by another.

S – is for Synthesis. "PAUSE" allows enough time and space to distill and synthesize information. This helps you in your immediate communication needs, but also helps you step away to gain perspective so you can see a larger picture. You can then look at the larger context of the situation and determine your strategy, plan or action. So much information comes at you so quickly, you would benefit from making time to step away from the chaos and letting go of what is not useful. This time to evaluate helps you to see what opportunities may be present that you might not otherwise have seen. This is important whether you are a CEO of a company, a working parent juggling home and work, or anyone who manages multiple roles or technologies.

E – is for Expression. After taking a moment, or an hour, or whatever length of time is necessary as your pause, you are better able to express your desires, goals or to articulate your feelings in a way that is more accurate and can be received by others. An additional bonus is that your expression feels more authentic, more powerful and centered.

Consider the Power of Pause! In a society where stopping is seen as non-productive, try to adjust your mindset to consider that there are times when not doing may be the most productive thing you could do.

"I wish we were not so single-minded about keeping our lives moving, and for once could do nothing, perhaps a huge silence might interrupt this sadness of never understanding ourselves and of threatening ourselves with death."
~Pablo Neruda

The Power of BIG Pause

P – is for Patience.
A – is for Allow.
U – is for Understand.
S – is for Synthesis.
E – is for Expression

*T*he Power of Pause is a methodology that can be used on a daily basis to create space for oneself in order to make good decisions, to communicate better, to receive more. Now the BIG Pause.

I have a dear friend, Phil Hough, who epitomizes the BIG Pause. His e-mail moniker is "nowhere man"... though perhaps it should be "everywhere man." Here is a wonderful man who truly LIVES. He and his partner work for a number of years, and then they go hiking for extended periods of time. They are true explorers. They have been up and down the Appalachian Trail; they have been to South America, recently to the British Isles. He stays in touch by e-mail and via his Web site. They have "settled" in Idaho, and really, it is a beautiful "home base".

So what is the BIG Pause? It is a kind of "time in" as opposed to a punitive "time out". It is a time to journey inward to look at where you have been and where you want to go, in a deep and profound manner. Many other cultures have BIG pauses integral to their cultures...for example; there is the Vision Quest, a Native American tradition.

In other cultures there are retreats and rites of passage to honor our transitions. Americans do not have this concept embedded in our culture. Immediately we conjure up all kinds or reasons we cannot do this. Taking a break spontaneously or planned without your cell phone, computer and BlackBerry, with an intention to be still doesn't require extensive time or planning. It could as easily happen at home as at a formal retreat. A BIG pause is filled with nothingingness. It allows you to reconnect to your natural flow, whether it means waking up without an alarm clock, eating lunch at 3pm instead of noon or going for a long walk in the middle of the day simply because you are moved to do so.

One client encountered this experience of nothingness on a trip to Maine. She discovered what she called "an inner, quiet space". This is a great description of the stillness that opens us to reconnecting with our soul and it is frequently in nature that we access this stillness.

The big Pause. Enter into your natural state and into your inner landscape for the greatest and most important journey - a journey to your essential Self. Be an explorer, be a child, as my mother says, *"con ojos como si acaba de nacer"* (with the eyes of a newborn). Who knows who you will find, waiting there for you?

"Listen. Make a way for yourself inside yourself.
Stop looking in the other way of looking."
~ Jelaluddin Rumi

The Reset Button

*I*t is so interesting, how busy we all are. We have all these modern gadgets that are supposed to help us get more done in less time. Personally, what I find is that they work more as tethers than tools. They keep us hooked to our work and they keep us from having real downtime, mentally as well as physically.

How many of us go away on vacation and bring our tool chest of cell phone, laptop, PDA, or at least we find out what the hotel's fax number is and if they have an Internet connection nearby? Our schedules are loaded to the gills, making sure that every hour, even every minute is filled to capacity, to ensure that we are indeed "not goofing off," but making the most of our time. We struggle to take time out to have lunch, take a walk, take a break even, let alone get out into the open air to just sit.

Just sit? What, and do "nothing"? Sacrilege! Paradoxically, that is what we need so often. It often happens that something is said by a client that appears simple yet it catches my attention and remains with me for a period of time, gestating, until it evolves into something more and deeper.

Recently, a client of mine was telling me about a bad week she was having. She is a mom, writer, musician and adventurer of the heart, but she is human and still has to manage everyday life. She had become frazzled with the unexpected events of her week and had a kind of "meltdown" as she called her situation. She described to me that out of this situation, she hit her "reset button".

Being a mom, we both related how that "reset button" can apply to small children. When my infant son would cry inconsolably in the middle of the night, the only thing that would calm him would be to take him outside in the cool (early morning) hours. The breeze or change of temperature or environment served to break the crying cycle so that he would calm down and return to sleep. My client does a similar thing with her young daughter.

After our talk, I realized the need to be aware of our ability to use the "reset button". How often do you run through your day as if you were on a treadmill two notches too high for you? How often in your day do you move from one task to another or mini-crisis to mini-crisis without taking a "pause" or breath for yourself? How does your body feel at the end of the day? If you could, would you like to scream and cry uncontrollably like an infant? If you are noticing these feelings, it is time to find your personal "reset button" and use it!

Take a walk outside if things at home or work are heading you into overwhelm. Go lie down and just breathe, even if it is only for a couple of minutes. Schedule a workout between your workday and going home to create a "pause" between your work and family life. Be creative about how you might create your personal "reset button". It will serve to break the cycle of run, run, run. It will create a space for you to breathe again, for your body to regain its energy without plugging into your adrenal system for the "fight or flight" response.

Next time you begin to feel out of control, with the symptoms of overwhelm and tightness in your body, remember the "reset button". If you can't switch to "off" it is the next best thing to regain your personal, emotional, physical and mental balance.

Happiness Is

I have been thinking about this concept, happiness,
for a while. What is happiness? What makes a
person happy? What does it mean to be happy?

I have created my 10 Principles of Happiness. They
have been honed from hundreds of coaching sessions and
discussions with friends and colleagues. Here they are:

1. No one is responsible for your happiness. No one
"gives" you happiness. It sources from you.

2. Happiness does not arise from the events in your
life. Instead it is constructed as a response to the
events in your life. Therefore…

3. You get to choose or not choose happiness. You
can choose to stay stuck in an unpleasant situation,
or you can move on, or you can transform your interpretation of what is happening so that you can accept
it and take a stance to create something from whatever has occurred.

4. There are things that have you feel happier and
things that make you feel lousy. It makes sense to do
more of the former and less of the latter.
Incorporating your body, mind and soul makes these
activities more meaningful and potent.

5. When in doubt, help somebody else. When you
become too self-involved, you are not happy. Know
that nothing in the world allows you to get in touch

with your own happiness than helping someone else. Service is a road to happiness.

6. Happiness is not a BIG deal; often it is in the little details of life that you feel the happiest. Petting your dog, swimming in the ocean, eating a sweet strawberry, listening to music, having a pillow fight with the family, all come to mind.

7. Why wait for happiness when you can be happy now? Too often you'll say "I'll wait until the weekend, until next year, until the kids are grown up, until we retire", etc. Why not be happy now?

8. Happiness has to do with how you make meaning and find purpose. It means that you have to pay attention so that you can be here now, in order to notice and to be happy.

9. If you don't remember a time when you were truly happy, it doesn't mean you weren't. It means you can't remember and probably should concentrate on being happy today, not being happy about yesterday. Which brings me to the 10th happiness principle.

10. Happiness lives in the now, not in the past nor in the future. Happiness is about BEING more than doing. Looking for it "out there" doesn't work. It is available here, now, alone or in company. Choose happiness!

"Life is made of moments, small pieces of glittering mica in a long stretch of gray cement. It would be wonderful if they came to us unsummoned, but particularly in lives as busy as the ones most of us lead now, that won't happen. We have to teach ourselves how to live, really live…to love the journey, not the destination."
~Anna Quindlen in A Short Guide to a Happy Life

Glittering Moments

She was on her way home from Wal-Mart. Her mind was on the vacation she was going to be taking in Nantucket. In two days she would be in a house full of adults and children, packing up lunches for a day at the beach. She never saw the car. She never felt the blow. She died instantly.

Do you know at any given moment that you will make it to tomorrow, to next week, to retirement or to any other point in the future? You don't know. You don't really think about it because if you were to think about it, you might decide that now is the time to make some changes. Not later, not when you have kids or when they grow up or when you retire. You might realize that each moment gone is a moment you will not recover. You might understand that words unspoken will forever linger in silence.

Look at how you are spending your moments. Have you recognized that the choices you make day-to-day will define the quality of your life? Anne Dillard writes, "How we spend our days is how we live our lives." We seem to be disconnected from the whole of our lives, living as if life were made up of compartments. First there are the compartments of the arenas of our lives. The work compartment, the marriage compartment, the friends compartment, etc. Then the temporal compartments: school time, college, adulthood and work, retirement, if, when, etc. We live as if each arena and time-frame were singular, just one step toward the time when we will "really be happy".

I would suggest that you not wait. I suggest you ask yourself, "Is this the way I want to spend this moment? Is this action, decision, behavior bringing me joy, well being, closer to what really matters in my life?" Deeply inquire into these questions and listen to the answers.

Here are some other ways of asking yourself these powerful questions:

- What do I want to be known for?

- If I don't play my own music, who will?

- What five words do I want people to use to describe me? What in my life needs to be expressed that is still not being expressed?

- As a child, what dream did I hold that has been forgotten?

- What wild and wonderful thing would I do or do again that would get me in touch with sheer, unadulterated joy?

Moments. Glittering moments. Like dew on the leaves in the morning, they evaporate. And the same identical moment will never be again. Don't waste these moments on things that don't matter. Live your life now!

"Turn your face to the sun and the shadows fall behind you."
~Maori Proverb

If I Had Time

July 21, 2004

I write firmly ensconced on a little island in Maine. Today it is cloudy, a bit wet. This morning, I stood on the rocks on the far side of the island and breathed in the salt air while the wind whipped my face with spray and cool. The loons and seagulls did not seem to mind. I just stood there, not trying to hide from Nature but willingly allowing her to envelop me with whatever was offered. It felt wonderful. I found myself thinking that I could do this each and every day if I stayed here. I imagined that each day I would walk along the rocky shore with my dog, feeling the spray, listening to the booming sound of waves breaking on ageless, rough rocks. Some days I would walk in bright sunshine, just as yesterday was. The cool ocean breeze would temper the heat from the sun. Other days, stormy skies might nudge me out from under my blankets for a walk to witness what Power truly looks and feels like, not the power of mankind, so often misused and selfish, but the power of the natural world, naked and honest in its caress as in its brute force. I could do this each day, that is, if I had time…

Later today, I sat listening to Sarah McLachlan, quietly sipping my coffee. I listened to the words and replayed the CD several times. I surrendered to the music, closing my eyes and imagining the music rocking me gently. I rose only to put another favorite CD into the player, Dido. She sang, "If my life is for rent, and I don't learn to buy, I deserve nothing more than I get, because nothing I have is truly mine." In a way, I see how this is true for me. I am here, for a minute period in "time", borrowing the things I have or believed I acquired in this lifetime. I realize that what truly belongs to me is not outside me, it is inside me. It is who I am in the world, the relationships I have, and the difference I may make for an individual in our time here. I had forgotten what it was like for me to listen to beautiful music, not in the background, but as the focus of my non-activity. I so wish that I could do this more often; that is if I had time...

Last night, when the house was dark and quiet, I lay in my bed reading a book of poetry by Mary Oliver, "Why I wake early". She is one of my favorite poets. Her ability to see the extraordinary in our ordinary activities, like waking each morning, or putting flowers in a vase, or finding an arrowhead during her walk, inspires me to pay attention to the world around me now. It reminds me to savor all of it, with all my senses, to drink in life, all of it, even the uncomfortable. I was content, reading in the quiet, lost in the world of Oliver's poetry, and wondered how I could do this more often. How I would enjoy quietly reading poetry for the sake of the poetry itself. I remember as I child how often I would enter my imagination, through music or prose or poetry or walks along the shore – and I would do so if I had time...

This afternoon, my son and husband ventured off island while I remained behind, to write this essay. I took a short break to make myself a late lunch. I made my lunch with great purpose, carefully picking out what food I would eat and how I might prepare it. There was no rush, and because of this I savored the meal, eating slowly. Normally I may read the paper or do something else between bites, but not today. Today on the porch I ate slowly and deliberately, imagining that this food, carefully prepared, would nourish me as much from the ingredients as the manner in which it was prepared. And I thought, wouldn't it be nice if each day I could take a break and thoughtfully prepare my food and my activities, with great purpose and with the intention of having all my moments nourish me – that is, if I had time...

"People say that what we're all seeking is a meaning for life...
I think that what we're really seeking is an experience of being
alive, so that our life experiences on a purely physical plane
will have resonance within our innermost being and reality,
so that we can actually feel the rapture of being alive.
~ Joseph Campbell

Finding Meaning, Creating Meaning

*W*ord of the devastation caused by the tsunami and earthquake in Thailand, Sri Lanka, India and Asia reached us through radio and television in December 2004. We saw life and death depicted in moving pictures. I couldn't help but wonder about the child on the beach, one moment playing and the next swept away by the wall of water; or the villagers that could not be reached, or any of the witnesses to the force of Nature. I wonder what their lives meant, to them, to me, to anyone. I wonder what my life means, to me, to you or to anyone.

Joseph Campbell said we are all seeking meaning. I see this in my daily conversations with people. Where does one go to seek meaning? Where does one look to find meaning? And how would one recognize it if one "found" it? Meaning is spoken of in terms of being lost or found, like it is an object outside of us. If it is outside of us, if it is something to be found, then what happens when we cannot find it out there? Does that make our lives meaningless? And who decides whether your life or my life has meaning or not?

Imagining myself on the beach in Phuket that December I saw myself in that final moment asking myself these questions. In that long moment I recognize that no, there is no meaning to be found, because meaning is not lost, not to me. There is nothing to be found, for I have not lost nor searched and found meaning – I have created it for myself. It is not something outside of me, it is within me and it is not lost but perhaps sometimes forgotten or taken for granted or shrouded in a kind of fog. I do not "find" meaning; I "create" meaning. And in that statement is an inner force much stronger than the raging waters of a tsunami or the shaking of the earth. I am at choice to decide what is meaningful to me and how or even if I will spend my life directed by that which I value and I have created for myself as meaningful. In that statement I decide how I will live my life, each and every moment – even until that final, long moment.

How are you living all your moments? Have you taken the time to understand yourself well enough to create and then to live your "meaning"? Don't look for it as if it were lost out there. It is not out there – it is within you, created by you. You and only you decide. Uncover it now, remember it now or re-create now. If not now, when?

(With gratitude and great respect and dedicated to the victims of the tsunami and earthquake whose circumstances gave me pause to ask these questions.)

Hiatus:
a pause or a gap in a series,
sequence or process

Hiatus

*T*here was a time I stopped writing EveryDay Epiphanies. To be truthful, it felt like writer's block, or to be even a bit more truthful, it felt like overwhelm. I do believe that life and work was "overwhelmingly" good and that although I was paying attention to the "good" I missed the "overwhelmingly" until I – figuratively – dropped.

It occurs to me that I expect overwhelm when things are going poorly. Something negative might happen and I become immersed in managing the situation or handling the problem. And that may lead to overwhelm. Somehow, I can justify needing a break when a struggle is involved.

But what happens when things are wonderful? Being a mother, I immediately think of the first months that I spent with a newborn. What a wonderful event his birth was! Everyone expected me to be happy, and I was. But it quickly turned to overwhelm and I felt too guilty to admit it. Fortunately for me, I have a wonderful partner who did notice and helped me sleep and take time for myself.

It is not that much different with work. Life is good. Lots and lots of good…and then it hit me. Even in the good times, it is OK, and even necessary, to take a hiatus or break. Sometimes I need to let some things go for a while, as much as I enjoy them. I have purposely made breaks in my calendar so I can return to my center; that still place, the only place immune to overwhelm.

What made me think that overwhelm only came from the negative? I don't know. I have learned that overwhelm can also occur from too much of a good thing as well (unless it is chocolate or ice cream). What were the signs? Now that I think back, they were there, only more subtle. Look at these and see if they are in your life too:

- An appointment that unexpectedly cancels causes feelings of relief

- Feeling a bit resentful that others are at the beach on a beautiful day while I am working

- Putting a book I want to read by the bed; unopened for a week

- Snapping at people I love without knowing why

- My to do list begins to produce offspring in the form of post-its

- I keep forgetting…what was that?

- People express awe when they view my calendar

If any of these sound familiar, "pause" and take a look at how much you are doing. You may be on the verge of "over-whelmingly good". Take a break, even in the good times. You will return refreshed and renewed.

"Look at every path closely and deliberately. Try it as many times as you think necessary. Then ask yourself and yourself alone one question. This question is one that only a very old man asks. My benefactor told me about it once when I was young and my blood was too vigorous for me to understand it. Now I do understand it. I will tell you what it is: "
Does this path have a heart?" If it does,
the path is good. If it doesn't, it is of no use."
~ Don Juan

Your Courageous Conversation

Every year I evaluate where I have been and even more importantly, where I want to go in the next year. I don't know about you, but each year that goes by feels as if it flies by more quickly than the one before. I imagine all the things I wanted to do and I tend to focus on what didn't get done instead of what did get done. Traditionally, with a new year come those awful New Year's Resolutions. I don't believe in New Year's resolutions. I do believe that in the absence of formal rituals, we may still use the New Year as a catalyst for a conversation about who we are and who we want to be.

As human beings, we evolve. We may sense that a change is imminent yet this may only be an intuitive sense. I suggest that it is more a remembering of who we are or a coming home to self. And from there, asking, "How do I want to engage in life authentically and fully? How much closer can I get to the thing that makes my soul sing? How can I more fully be ME when so much of the world is encouraging me to be someone else?" As David Whyte, the poet inquires, "What is the courageous conversation I am refusing to have with myself, in my own heart and mind with regard to my work and the present life threshold on which I find myself? What is the courageous conversation I am not having with my partner or spouse, my children or loved ones?"

Note, he says, "refusing to have". The implication is that we are aware of the conversation and we are moving fearfully and actively away from it despite the acknowledgement that it is there waiting.

Now is the time to ask yourself these questions, if you have not already done so because time is flying by. Each moment that passes is a moment that will never again be recovered. Is that really how you want to live your moments, your life? Because if it is not, what are you waiting for? The joke is on us, thinking that there will always be time to take that trip, to reconcile with a friend, to have a job we love, to travel, to do any number of a hundred things. Life is terminal. We just forget until something dramatic happens that wakes us up to this reality. I don't mean this to be morbid. I do mean it to be NOW.

The first step in moving toward your true self and future is to decide to do so; to make a commitment, in every cell of your body, to listen to the song in your soul and to act upon it. Decide. Take a stand. Make a public declaration about who you really are. I promise you, the Universe begins to fling doors open when you make this kind of profound declaration.

Start with a blueprint, much like architectural blueprints made for a house that will be built. Write it out - in the present tense as if it were happening right now. Write what you really want, not what you think you can have. As humans we will always want to take the path of least resistance.

Fill in your blueprint with as much detail as you can and add to it as you go along. Ask yourself, what would I be doing, how would I be behaving, what actions would I be taking, if I were now this person I want to be? Then your challenge is to begin to live this way as if it were true now. You begin to melt into your future once you begin to live as if it were so. This occurs more organically, with less struggle, more intuitively. It combines a kind of flow with, but without the attachment to the structures (like using an architects plan and choosing the right building materials) that will support the building of your future. The shift moves from making it happen to allowing it to happen. Take note, it will only happen when you purposely *decide* that you will move into your authentic life. Not decide mentally, but whole-heartedly, to move in the direction of your Self. And it starts with a courageous conversation, and frankly, with faith.

Someone I know recently said, "If you feel safe, you're not living a bigger game...Go for the thing that makes you go 'gulp!'" What makes you go "gulp"? Therein lies a clue to what is next for you.

Winter is a time for moving inward. Reflect during this time on how you want to live. Listen to the inner wisdom of your heart and soul. And then, after you have had your courageous conversation with yourself, decide, declare and do. After all, it's your life and no one else's.

*"Wisdom emerges in the gap between
the question and the answer."*
~ Tobin Hart in Teaching for Wisdom

Powerful Questions

We are intrigued by questions and burdened by the need to have the right answer. If you are like most people you are uncomfortable with ambiguity so you drive for the answers. Yet the right question, at the right moment, can be surprisingly powerful, a catalyst for epiphany and action. Coaches spend much of their training honing their skill of asking powerful questions and moderating this skill with intuition to determine the best timing and most effective approach to a question for a client.

Here are some questions for you to see if any of these resonate with your own inner wisdom and to give voice to some of the silent questions that may be living in you. It is my hope that at least one of these questions will have you pause long enough to listen to the answer that may have been waiting for the arrival of the right question.

• Are you taking the path of least resistance or are you choosing what you really want?

• What would you do if you could not fail?

• What is the courageous conversation you are not having - with yourself, with others?

• What do you need to let go of so you can move on?

• What is the question living in you that needs to be asked?

- Are you being true to yourself? If not, what do you choose to do about it?

- Who inspires you? For what reasons?

- Are you expending your energy in avoiding situations and conflict or creating new possibilities?

- Where in your life are you resigned? What will it take to change that?

- What are you struggling with the most (really)?

- What about the past are you not able to accept? What would it take to let it go or to accept the past and present as it is?

- Tension exists between what we want and what it is. Where is your tension?

- If you were to take one powerful step towards your own greatness what would that be?

- If you were five times bolder, what would you be doing now?

- What five people in your life can you depend on and for what?

- Who in your life demonstrates qualities you would like to emulate?

- What keeps you away from the thing you love (to do, to have)?

- What would bring you towards the things you love (to do, to have)?

- What is the response to "who am I?"

- What is your response to "why am I here?"

- What is your response to "what do I stand for?"

- What is the question you want to be asked?

- What am I choosing out of fear?

- What am I choosing out of faith?

- What am I choosing out of love?

- What am I choosing out of wisdom?

- What am I choosing out of power?

- How does my passion manifest itself?

- Where in my life could I use help?

- Five years from now what would I say about my life to an old friend who I run into?

- What do I believe about myself and how does that move me forward or hold me back?

- What do I truly want my life to orient around (like planets orient around the sun)?

- What makes me smile?

- What makes me laugh?

- Who do I need to tell that I love them?

- What do I need for my spiritual well being that I am not now doing or getting?

- Where or when do I feel most connected to myself?

- Where or when do I feel most connected to others?

- Where or when do I feel most connected to God or to the divine (as you define it)?

There are many more possible questions. Some may not have answers, some may not have answers <u>yet</u>. Boldness is asking the question even if the answer scares you.

Paradox:
A statement or proposition that
despite sound (or seemingly sound) reasoning
from acceptable premises leads to a conclusion
that seems senseless, logically unacceptable
or self-contradictory.

A Perfect Paradox

When you are struggling, feeling that your life is either out of control or if you have had several setbacks and are feeling "beat up"...consider the following questions, slowly and thoughtfully: What if life is perfect just the way it is right now, without any need to change anything? How would you be living your life? Really, consider that everything in your life is just right. Don't resist what is. Don't try to change it. If it is perfect just the way it is, what would be possible? What would it allow you to do?

When you struggle and resist what is, you miss whatever possibilities may be in the space between what is and what you want it to be. It is in this space where you choose suffering or ease. The more you resist, the more you suffer. Sometimes there is more power in the surrender than in the fight. Sometimes the true warrior must embrace "what is" in order to be ready for her future victory. The Paradox may be that to win sometimes you must surrender.

Joseph Campbell, the renowned mythologist puts it this way: "We're in a free fall into the future. We don't know where we're going. Things are changing so fast. And always when you're going through a long tunnel, anxiety comes along. And all you have to do to transform your hell into a paradise is to turn your fall into a voluntary act. It's a very interesting shift of perspective...Joyfully participate in the sorrows of the world and everything changes." Can you imagine your "fall as a voluntary act"? What if you were to stop any resistance to what is occurring in your life right now. Stop any resistance even if it scares you. What if you came to accept what is in your life right now? Could you look at this as one step on your journey and not the final destination? Could you conceive that what is happening right now, unknown to you at this moment, may take you to exactly where you need to be in the future? What freedom could there be in this?

I learned this lesson from a friend of mine who lost everything she owned in a fire. She and her husband escaped with their lives. Over drinks about a year after the fire she told me that losing everything had given her both great sorrow and a great sense of freedom – there were no attachments to anything and she was free to create something completely new and aligned with how she wanted her life to be. I thought she showed amazing courage – and amazing insight!

What if your life is perfect, just as it is right now? Asking this question takes faith and courage. What is available to you in this situation right now that you might not have access to otherwise? You may find that despite what is occurring, this may be the catalyst for a wonderfully fulfilling life adventure, if you can stop struggling and resisting what is.

"Life has meaning only if one barters it day by day
for something other than itself."
Antoine de Saint-Exupery

Looking for Meaning in All the Wrong Places

Not long ago at a conference I attended I heard a speaker talk about the future and who or what type of person might be the new "most likely to succeed" person.

He claimed that tapping into the "right side of the brain" – the side that synthesizes information rather than analyzes it, the side that focuses on context more than content, would be the future of the way we work. There are some real economic reasons for this shift but I see it as something more profound. He noted that as a culture we have achieved more materially, including greater wealth, yet our satisfaction with our lives has not increased. We have not been able to buy happiness. Indeed, for many, more means more complicated.

What I hear now in conversations is the word "simplify". Do you feel like you are spinning out of control with all that you do and have? Like planets without the sun, there is nothing to keep you from flying around wildly if you don't know your purpose, if you don't know yourself.

What you may be looking for is meaning in your life, a sense of purpose and connection to something greater than yourself. You jump from job to job, relationship to relationship, from one self-help book to another. Looking for what?

It is a connection to something inside yourself that makes you feel alive. It is the connection with the soul. That is the source of passion and commitment. When you are connected to that, work no longer feels like work. You are in harmony with yourself and with the world around you. There is no looking for something; you are in it.

What is that for you? Do you find yourself constantly looking "out there" for your answers? What if you looked "in here" for your answers? What if it really weren't that complicated?

Go into your interior world to be quiet so you can listen to your soul voice. Your answer is here inside. Not out there somewhere. Be still - so that you can come alive.

"Do not let your fire go out, spark by irreplaceable spark, in the hopeless swamps of the approximate, the not-quite, the not-yet, the not-at-all. Do not let the hero in your soul perish, in lonely frustration for the life you deserved, but have never been able to reach... The world you desired can be won. It exists, it is real, it is possible, it is yours."
~Ayn Rand

Evolving: A Message From My Soul Voice

I have mentioned your soul voice before. It is that little whisper that you hear distinctly when you don't censor. It is the voice that gives you the very first answer to a profound question. The soul voice does not intellectualize or rationalize. The soul voice tells you exactly the way it is for you whether you want to hear it or not.

Your life evolves, work changes, relationships wane and grow. Catalysts such as birth, death, marriage, divorce, happy and sad occasions, can move you out of your sleep and awaken profound questions in you. It is when you find yourself in the gap, between what was and what will be, that you experience discomfort, and the inevitable transitions become apparent. This is the time to listen to that soul voice. It will provide direction that aligns with your most authentic self.

In trying times you may choose the path of least resistance. The world is busy telling you how you cannot and should not want what you want or dream your dreams. You decide that the time is not yet right - when you have more money, when the kids are grown, later, later. And too many times, later never does arrive. Ask yourself, if not now, when? At least begin now to work for what you truly want in your life.

Here are some ways of bridging the gap between where you have been and where you want to be. Use these tips to keep your dreams alive and to begin working toward a complete manifestation of who you are and what you want for your life and/or business.

- **Stay focused.** Do something each day, regardless of how small, to keep your actions moving toward the realization of your dreams or the vision of your business.

- **Get Support.** Choose to surround yourself with positive people who will act as sounding boards and cheerleaders. This is especially helpful when you are losing momentum or are confronted with obstacles.

- **Write it, draw it, and breathe life into it.** I am a firm believer in creating a blueprint for what you want, whether it is to write it down, or draw a picture, or have your own personal theme song. Choose something tangible that you can experience or touch each day to remind you of what matters to you.

- **Set appropriate goals.** When you set your goals according to what holds the most meaning for you, then you move forward with greater ease. Don't set goals based on what you think you should do, but instead keep the vision in mind and ask yourself what about that goal will move you closer to the realization of that vision. Then take action.

- **Allow yourself victories.** Don't set your goals or standards so high that you cannot meet them. This sets you up for failure. Set yourself up for success instead. Benchmark goals so you can anticipate the feeling of accomplishment and so you are not so overwhelmed that you take no action at all.

• **Remove tolerations and energy drains.** Take a good look at what drains you. If you are tolerating someone or something remove it from your life find a solution to dealing with it. This frees up your time and energy and opens up a more positive outlook for you.

• **Don't beat yourself up.** If things don't go according to plan, resolve the issue as much as you can, then move on and forward. Don't be the person on a diet who in the middle of their diet plan binges on ice cream, feels guilty, then gives up completely because of that one binge.

• **Honor where you have been.** There is much to be said for the wisdom that is born of past experiences. Don't throw that out. Sift through your experiences and use what you can from the past to create your future. Let go of anything that is habitual and no longer serves you.

• **If you are struggling, change course.** Honestly, life really doesn't have to be a struggle all the time. Remember, things may well be difficult but not a struggle. If you really want something your vision for your desired future will take you through difficult situations without feeling like you are struggling. Struggle has an emotional component that includes hopelessness and a sense of disempowerment. Difficulty is just that without the hopelessness and disempowerment.

• **What if exactly where you are were perfect?** Many times when clients are uncomfortable or stuck in their present situation I ask them this question: "What is the opportunity here?" Or "If where you are right now were perfect, what would you be able to do or have that you couldn't otherwise do or have?" This allows you to shift your focus to the possibilities that are inherent in every situation. By doing this it options you may not have considered become available to you. Big shift!

Because you are always evolving you will experience transitions throughout your life. There are catalysts that will demand that you enter transitions abruptly. And there are also slow, steady shifts that will begin to change you quietly. In either case, keep your sights set beyond the gap between where you are now and where you want to be. Plot your course with intention using your soul voice as the navigator for your evolution.

Chapter Two
Family, Friends and Community

"Whoever finds love beneath hurt and grief disappears into emptiness with a thousand new disguises."
~Jelaluddin Rumi

Fearlessness

*I*t seems that lately everyone is talking about fear and those things that keep us at a heightened state of alert. Individuals cannot consistently remain in this kind of fight or flight state without damaging their well being on many levels.

September 11th propelled many individuals into recognizing an acute tension, which has been there all along. I noticed a surge in the numbers of people coming to coaching right after this date. People recognized that they could achieve more if they had the right support and that time was now to lead a fulfilling life. In the absence of support, many others remain imagining their dreams of success or envisioning the business they may one day own or the life they may one day lead. Coaching is one of the few modalities where you can find someone who will help you enlist the courage to go after your dreams.

People also come to coaching when the pain in their lives is so acute that they can bear it no longer. The option to actually explore their lives- both the shadow and light- becomes more compelling than remaining in the same lifestyle. The fear that has held them hostage and has kept them from taking any steps toward being fully alive is replaced by the fear that one day they may die never having lived at all.

There is a gap between what is and what could be. You may fill the gap with temporary pleasures. For some it is food, for others it is a variety of -isms (alcoholism, workaholism, etc). You may medicate the discomfort in an effort to avoid facing a life not fully lived. You may create reasons why you cannot do what it is you really want to do. You may have a lifetime of building belief systems that set you up to fail, that tell you to be afraid. These beliefs protect you from yourself. They are a temporary oasis in a desert with no horizon, no boundaries. They may serve you well for a long time. They keep you safe…until something happens and you experience a different sort of death.

Paradoxically, as the fear of everyday violence erupts, another fear is expelled. That is the fear of connection between you and your inner self, as well as between you and the rest of your community. During disasters you may have witnessed the outpouring of help in so many ways from so many people. There is heroism everywhere. People respond by connecting, running home to their family and friends, to embrace and be together both in sorrow and in thanks.

Compassion comes from your ability to share the pain you feel with others. Soften around the discomfort you find between what is and what could be, between self and ego, between you and another person. If you are able to relate to this place, it may allow you to see clearly a special aspect of yourself. You may identify false assumptions and limiting beliefs. You may treat yourself and others with more compassion. It takes fearlessness to connect to your true self and to share yourself with others. It is fearlessness that allows you to show compassion even when you feel anger, or to remain open even when you wish to barricade yourself into sturdy walls.

If you can remain with the uncertainty and not attempt to camouflage it, you may finally see yourself clearly and with confidence. This is the gap between dreaming of your potential and realizing it. Visit this place inside of you and return a fearless warrior.

"It is what it is."
~Gameboy Guru, Joseph Connolly,
Six years old

Gameboy Guru:
It is What It is

My son and I like to make cookies. (He likes to bake, but mostly he likes to eat cookie dough and make a mess.) During one of our bake-a-thons I inadvertently knocked over the bag of flour. Muttering a number of expletives to myself, I also exclaimed, "I wish I could just make this mess go away!"

Without missing a beat, Joseph quietly said, "Mom, it is what it is." "What?" I asked. He repeated, "It is what it is, Mom. It's a mess so we just have to clean it up, that's all."

This Gameboy Guru woke me up. Still, unbelieving, I asked him, "Joseph, did you hear someone say that or read that somewhere?" "No, Mom, I just know. And I also know that people are what they are, and they do what they do. It's all really quite simple." he added matter-of-factly. Yoda had taken over my son's body, I am sure.

In that moment I realized that I had been elsewhere while making the cookies. My mind had been on all the things I thought I had left undone and waiting. I became aware of tightness in my body and stress that I was carrying, even into this most pleasant activity. It occurred to me that a major source of stress comes from wanting things to be what they are not. That if I could accept things just as they were, not only could I deal with them more appropriately, but I would not be experiencing the tension that exists between "what is" and "what I want it to be". (I knew that, after all I AM a coach!)

How often do you find yourself wishing that things were different? Not only wishing they were different but also actually behaving as if they were what you wanted them to be. You may be ignoring the truth of what is because it is painful, inconvenient, uncomfortable, more work, scary even. Does this serve you? Does it make sense to put your energy into the fantasy of what you wish it could be instead of addressing what is right in front of you? Would you struggle less if you were accepting of what is instead of operating based on what you wish it were?

I am not saying you shouldn't dream or strive for something better for yourself. If anything, looking forward or dreaming gives you the focus to achieve the task or manifest the dream. But if you don't accept what is, just as it is, you will never know how to plot your course, or see the hidden opportunities or create the appropriate steps to get to your dream or vision. Instead, your steps will be directed toward an illusion.

If your business is slow, don't blame the economy. Instead, accept things have slowed down and admit, "My sales are down now." That is the first step in increasing sales. Why? Because you may now have time to re-evaluate strategies that have not been working because of the many economic fluctuations. It allows you to plan, re-focus, streamline operations, and produce better marketing materials. You may notice gaps that you were not aware of. But none of this occurs, if we first don't accept what is.

You may be ignoring signs in your relationships that indicate an unhealthy relationship. Relationships are an area of great imagination. At first you may see only each other's virtues. Then you may see only each other's faults. Finally, if you are committed to one another, you may see each other as you really are. It isn't until you arrive here that the friendship becomes solid.

"People are what they are and they do what they do." But how many relationships are based on such acceptance? Why do you want your significant other to be something that he/she is not? Why do you ask your children to grow up to someone else's expectations? For that matter, why is your relationship with yourself based on someone else's expectations or conditioning? Why do you deny your true self and keep yourself from your most authentic potential?

Joseph finished baking cookies that afternoon, laughing, eating cookie dough and making a mess. I forgot about what had been left undone (because thinking about it wasn't going to get it done and it was getting in the way of our creative cookie-making!)

Teachers come in all shapes and sizes. From my Gameboy Guru, here are Joseph's 7 Rules for Living. I hope he, and I, never forget them.

1. It is what it is.

2. Be exactly where you are and you will have more fun.

3. If it's a mess, just clean it up.

4. People are what they are.

5. People do what they do.

6. It's all really quite simple.

7. Regularly make cookies, eat dough, and get your hands yucky.

After all, isn't that what life is made for? Enjoy!

*"The quickest way for a mother to get a child's attention
is to sit down and answer the telephone."*
~Ginny Unser, in First Aid for a Mother's Soul

A Perfect Moment

"Can you cuddle with me?" he asks. It's 8:35 p.m. It's more than a half hour past his bedtime and school looms tomorrow.

This is after the nightly ritual of stalling. First pajamas that are too itchy, they need to be changed. Then the bathroom rituals, peeing and brushing of teeth and washing of hands. Time for bed. "I'm thirsty. This water is too warm. Can I have ice in it?" At last snuggled down with all his "guys", so many stuffed animals and critters I wonder how he fits into his bed. I sing him his "Goodnight Joseph" song. No night's sleep can begin without the comfort of his special song. I pull the covers over him, leaving the room as I wish him sweet dreams. Then he asks, "Can you cuddle with me?

I think of the dishes that need to be washed, the laundry that needs to be folded, the e-mail which needs response and the husband watching football wondering if I'll be back down or not. Then I allow myself to feel my soul's wish. "Aha!" my heart says, "a perfect moment!" I allow myself to recognize the question for what it really is, a request to connect, to express intimacy, an opportunity to nourish both our souls. I think about my day, the rushing around, and the intensity of my focus in my conversations, the giving, the taking, and the choices I have been making all day, all week. I am at another crossroads. I have been fortunate. My soul recognizes this perfect moment and tells me to choose wisely. I wonder how many moments I may have missed today in my juggling. Will I choose this one or will this one be lost forever?

"Can you cuddle with me, please? Two minutes?" Okay,

two minutes. "No, I meant five, no ten minutes." I lie down next to the wriggling bundle wondering if I won't fall asleep within ten minutes myself. We spoon together, his little body fitting back around his source, my abdomen, my womb. We warm each other. It feels like honey melting into warm milk. After some time, he turns his body to face me, throwing his arm around my neck and kissing my face. "I love my momma", he whispers as he pulls my face toward his with his little arm.

This perfect moment is ours. All the dishes, the laundry, the email, and even the football fan are forgotten in that instant of intimacy. "Of course I'll cuddle with you", I whisper silently, for as long as you want me to. What other answer is there?

"The Hundreth Monkey"

*I*n 1952, on the island of Koshima, scientists were providing Japanese monkeys with sweet potatoes dropped in the sand. A young monkey learned to wash them to avoid eating the sand. She taught this to her playmates, to her mother and to other monkeys. Scientists observed this behavior between 1952 and 1958.

Not all the adults washed the sweet potatoes during this time; only the adults who imitated their children would do so. In the autumn of 1958 a certain number of monkeys (99?) were washing sweet potatoes. Later that day one more monkey learned to wash the sweet potato- the 100th monkey. The scientists further observed that from this point on, colonies of monkeys on this island and in islands and on the mainland faraway now began washing their sweet potatoes. This is the story of the Hundredth Monkey.

I have no idea if this is fact or fiction. The story of the "Hundredth Monkey" comes from a book of the same name, published in 1981 by Ken Keyes, Jr., and it was written about the dangers of nuclear power and weapons. Mr. Keyes offers hope that if enough people come to really believe the horror and potential for devastation due to nuclear weapons, that we will, as a civilization, never allow this type of annihilation to happen. However, I couldn't help but think of this story in light of the global events of today. Constantly, I am being asked, and reading about, how we as individuals can contribute to peace, what can be done to resolve the issues breeding terrorism, and how it is that we as individuals can make a difference.

Many individuals come to coaches for the reason of transforming their lives to reflect greater meaning and purpose. Society with its agendas, both obvious and hidden, can frustrate many a well-intentioned person. Combined with an attitude of instant gratification, the long road of steady work and focus may be diverted to areas of greater material rewards, shortcuts and less personal satisfaction. But that can only last so long. Suddenly a catalyst, or an epiphany, surfaces which disrupts our worldview.

Allow me to return to the question of how we as individuals can make a difference. Allow me to tap into your imagination for an answer.

Imagine what our world would be like if each person handled their individual lives with integrity. Imagine if each person were to determine what he or she would define as his or her life purpose, and then, would focus on reaching the potential hidden inside. Imagine how world leaders, businesses and corporations, and everyday citizens, would make decisions if the value were less on wealth and more on the human condition. If politics focused on making peace instead of making war, what would be possible?

In his book Mr. Keyes speculates: "...when a certain critical number achieves an awareness, this new awareness may be communicated from mind to mind...there is a point at which if only one more person tunes in to a new awareness, a field is strengthened so that this awareness is picked up by almost everyone!" What would happen if "99" individuals focused on peace and harmony, and suddenly, one additional person re-framed their lives in a way to fully engage in their life in a positive manner? Could we achieve this kind of mass shift in consciousness that would transform our planet?

What can you do? Ask yourself:

Where am I in the counting? Am I stuck, in my life or business, in a former reality that is based on past assumptions as truth? What are those assumptions?

How can I challenge these assumptions for myself and those whose lives I affect? How will challenging these assumptions move me out of a stuck place and into a more creative and positive stance, better able to flow with the changes needed to sustain life in the world?

At what level am I living life? On a daily basis, am I on automatic pilot or am I aware of my connection to all, making choices on purpose?

How am I visioning my business to support my clients, my staff and myself? Do I handle myself with integrity, honestly and with thoughtfulness?

What do I need to do to align with my deepest values?

Listen carefully for those answers and make your choices in alignment with those answers. YOU. Don't look elsewhere for the decisions. This is about one person at a time designing their life and work around what truly matters.

I myself am holding out for the Hundredth Human Being. I am patiently awaiting the "shift" that occurs on the level of mass consciousness. I don't know if the plan is any more complicated than "handle your own stuff".

This is not going to happen at the level in which our problems were created. This will happen, I believe, much as it happened in Mr. Keye's story. But instead of monkeys washing their food, I am hoping humans will shift in their level of awareness and break open a creative force lying dormant, awaiting that critical number.

The Dawn After the Storm

*I*n September 2003 the Mid-Atlantic region was hit hard by Hurricane Isabel. The aftermath brought destruction of property and disruption of services. In Annapolis, known as a sailing mecca, the marinas and beach areas were damaged. Homes and businesses were flooded. Thousands of people were left without electricity for days and many were not able to use water as their wells had become contaminated. Businesses lost thousands of dollars as they were forced to close due to flooding and utility deprivation and employees were forced out of work as well.

As I look back on this and at other disasters a couple of things occur to me:

- I noticed the dependency we have developed upon technology. Without electricity, computers did not work and those with cable for Internet services were unable to communicate via e-mail. PDAs and cell phones could not be recharged. The connection to clients, friends and family was severed for a while. Everything was put on hold as people worked together to share resources and clean up. Collaborating was more useful than competition and indeed, strangers became neighbors as one house was hooked up to another to share electricity, phones and water.

- Many people realized that their business systems were not prepared to handle disastrous situations. There was no contingency or backup to business systems. Additionally, many businesses found that the lack of insurance or preventative measures ensured devastating outcomes during this time. What an awakening!

• We take much for granted. It isn't until we are not able to do things or have what we need, that we realize how important this is to us and how we need to protect the availability of services, maintain our business systems and indeed, nurture our relationships with our neighbors and business alliances.

What lessons can be learned from a violent act of nature? I am convinced that for every breakdown, an equally powerful breakthrough is available. Being creatures of habit, we tend to take the path of least resistance until one day, everything is shattered unexpectedly.

• First, we need to deal with the emotional aspects of breakdown. We tend to jump to action without considering emotions of fear, of loss and grief or even anger. Dealing with these up front and if needed allows healing which is as important as the tasks of recovery.

• Second, evaluate what back-up systems you need to put into place. We tend to take the simple things for granted – water, food and shelter. How can you plan you for these?

• Third, what is the nature and quality of your relationships? It is easy to take for granted the neighbor next door until a crisis brings you together.

• Fourth, what else in your life are you taking for granted? Take a good hard look at that one.

• Fifth, what reserves or cushion have you built into your life or business that could sustain a financial hit brought on by a natural or man-made occurrence? If you do not feel like you have reserves, chances are that when a crisis occurs, your fear will cloud your ability to deal with it. Be sure to build reserves for those times when you have to weather any kind of storm.

One more thing. The day the hurricane hit I noticed how the birds and insects became quieter and quieter until everything was silent. How is it that they know or sense impending disaster, and we so often do not? What are they paying attention to that we are not paying attention to?

The day following the storm I awoke to the sounds of birds singing, mixed with chain saw motors. It was a curious interposition to say the least. And as I walked onto my porch, and viewed so many trees in the backyard uprooted or downed, I also noticed the crispness in the air, the cleanliness of the day and the brightness of the sunshine. It was as if Mother Nature were demonstrating that if you can ride out the worst storm, another day would dawn bright and clean and there will be another chance to live and work. Don't take that gift for granted.

"A man went for a walk along the beach one morning after a storm. As far as the eye could see, the sand was littered with starfish that had washed up on the shore and were dying in the sun. In the distance, the man saw a young boy walking down the beach, picking up starfish after starfish, tossing them back into the surf one at a time. When he was close enough to be heard above the waves, the man asked, "Child, why are you doing this? There must be thousands of starfish out here…what possible difference can you make?" The boy reached down, picked up a starfish and threw it as far as he could back in to the sea. "Sure made a lot of difference to that one." And he reached down to pick up another.
~ The Starfish Story - Adapted from "The Star Thrower"
~ Loren Eisley"*

The Power of One

So many times we stop short of being helpful to another person, never realizing that through everyday or common actions we have an impact on another person or even on a larger group of people. My husband told me the story of Gerda Weissman Klein (*All But My Life*), a Holocaust survivor, who had endured unrelenting hardships and dehumanizing treatment. Upon her rescue from the camps, and just as she had given up hope, one of the rescuers, a soldier, held open the door for her to walk through. She tells of how that small and perhaps insignificant gesture restored her faith in humanity, her sense of dignity and hope. Sometimes, we just don't know how an action, so ordinary, can affect an individual, but when delivered with compassion and kindness, can change someone deeply.

Do you believe that indeed, you can really make a difference? Who are you, what power do you have to impact another individual? Can your existence really make a difference for anyone? At some point in your life you may begin to recognize a need to have your life truly matter. At that point, you may have accomplished much in the way of your material life and yet an uncomfortable sense of void or emptiness may be present.

Perhaps you experience an "epiphany" through a personal tragedy? Or something like 9-11 happens and you learn of the heroism of everyday people, who realized that they could make a difference for someone, whether it meant giving their lives for others or helping to heal the pain in the aftermath.

You have the ability, and even the responsibility, to make a difference for someone else. But you need to be open to the opportunity to do so. Whether it means helping an elderly person with luggage at the airport, or signing up for a Big Brother/Sister program or spending time with your own children, you make a difference. It might not make the papers or the news, you may be the only one aware of the gift you give or receive, but what matters is that you have been in touch with "The Power of One".

Look around and see what difference you can make for someone. Next time you see an opportunity to help another person, don't keep walking. Pause, and with kindness and compassion, give a little of yourself for someone else. You will feel differently afterwards. The Power of One affects not only the person receiving, but also the person giving. Be that person today.

"It is only with the heart that one can see rightly;
what is essential is invisible to the eye."
~ Antoine de Saint-Exupery

Gratitude

*D*o you ever notice how easy it is to rejoice in your good fortune when things are going well for you? How easy it is for you to be kind and generous when you feel all is right with our world?

But what happens when you experience set back? How far do you reach into a mindset of scarcity when you lose something? How much doubt enters when you are criticized or when circumstances do not conform to what you had expected? Who do you become when an unexpected shift in your life occurs? How frightened do you get when your safety net is abruptly removed and your complacency is challenged?

It may become increasingly difficult for you to value what you have when you feel that your lifestyle or beliefs have been compromised. Yet, it is during the dark moments that it becomes most essential to "see" the light in your life. A midnight sky is brightened by the small stars that can only appear in the darkest sky. It is your experience of the darkest night sky that allows you to see the twinkling light.

These are the times that open you to being vulnerable; a frightening proposition at best. Yet, consider that in being vulnerable you may also receive unexpected compassion and generosity and love. If you hurt, can you ask your friend to comfort you? Yes. If you are ill, can you request help? Yes. Would you otherwise connect to another person at this deep level in your every day life? Probably not. These are the times when you become aware of what you truly value. When the superficial is stripped away, when you no longer have the comforts that may deceive you from experiencing what truly matters to you, it is then that you are left with the essential elements that bring meaning to your life.

What matters to you? Is it your family, friends, skills and abilities, your grace and courage? Be grateful when you can see this so clearly. Be grateful for the closeness it brings in your relationships. Be grateful for the gift that you are. Surround yourself with people of integrity and people who share your values. Be grateful for your health. Be grateful for love in your life. Be grateful that you can use your body to dance and sing.

Take a moment, right now, and write down what you are grateful for. Not later, do it now.

If you are experiencing a dark night, look for the twinkling stars. I promise you, they are there. But your eye may not see them. Look with your heart.

"Friendship is a single soul dwelling in two bodies."
~ Aristotle

Time and Friendship

"Will I still know you when we're 40?" I asked. I was sitting on the floor of the telephone alcove in my dorm at college. The payphone and its shelf formed a "cubby" where I could wedge myself in an attempt to gain some privacy from the hallway.

"What do you think? Will we still be talking when we're forty?" I was speaking to my best friend, a young man named Gerry. It was the kind of question that only a naïve nineteen year old looking into some far away and uncertain future might ask. At the time, forty seemed like an eternity away with images of old age already setting in. Writing this, now closer to fifty than forty, I can't help but chuckle a bit remembering how I felt. For some reason this seemingly insignificant moment keeps replaying in my mind, as vivid as if I were still sitting in the cubby talking on the payphone to my friend, only a few dorms away. I think it replays for me because it has a lot to do with my feelings about friendship.

Gerry and I have been friends for over thirty years. We still see each other occasionally and we write back and forth a couple of times a year to catch up and just to check in. I saw him a couple of years at our college, where my friendship with him began. A dear friend who worked for the college had passed away. She had been like a second mother, always taking care of "her kids", inviting them to her farm, feeding us when we couldn't stand the cafeteria food any longer and generally giving us a place to call home when we needed it. We came to honor her memory and for me, it was a way to reconnect with a very important part of my life.

I had called Gerry to tell him of her passing. He agreed to meet me there. It is amazing how we picked up exactly where we left off regardless of time or distance. It is always the same, as if nothing really separated us, despite living in different locations, having our own families and living very different lives. He is still exactly the same as I remember him years ago, ageless in my relationship with him. In the moments that we do see each other, I see flashes of the many interactions we have had in our lives: joyous times, funny times and sad times.

I think this is what makes up friendship; this is it, all of it. It is the way you feel despite time and distance. It is the memories of the past and the anticipation of future exchanges. It is laughing, crying and sharing all of life even if it is one snippet at a time. It is the quiet knowing inside one another that recognizes the need to connect for no apparent reason. It is being close enough when silence is comfortable and words are superfluous. It is having a history with someone that involves the mind, body and spirit on profound levels. It is feeling that the tiniest things are special. (Something I will always remember is Gerry telling me that the hair on his arm always stands up when he reads my poetry. Now who but a really close friend would say that?)

Think about what friendship really means to you. Because true friendship is a precious gift that needs care and nurturing and support. It is not enough to say you're friends. True friendship, much like love, is an engagement of the soul. Ask yourself, whom in your life do you value as a true friend? What is it about that person that is special to you? What are you doing to nurture that friendship? And when was the last time you told that person what they meant to you, despite time, distance and all that busyness in our lives?

Friends are bridges between our past, present and future. Sitting in the alcove so many years ago, I think I may have sensed that. And in asking the question, I also knew the answer.

"The deeper that sorrow carves into your being the more joy you can contain. Is not the cup that holds your wine the very cup that was burned in the potter's oven?"
~ Kahlil Gibran

My Mother's Greatest Lesson

Statistics confirm that many of us in the Boomer generation are currently or will be dealing with taking care of our parents at the same time we take care of our children. I have coached several clients who have had to deal with this issue. My husband and his siblings dealt with a mother who was diagnosed with dementia, who lived many years with this before passing away. So this process is familiar to me; even more so now as I become one of the statistics.

I have always been extremely close to my mother. She has modeled for me great courage, compassion, unconditional love, generosity and what I call "ferocious love" for her children. It was these qualities that helped her survive the death of my father and bring up three teenagers that didn't turn out too badly.

Her life has been one of hardships, yet when I think of how she managed her life in a country where she didn't even speak the language much less understand the culture, the word that comes to mind is grace. She managed this mostly solo as my father died in 1976. When I look at her I see her history written on her face; the struggles have bent her but not broken her. Her eyes still dance when they see her grandchildren.

She has great difficulty remembering what was just said or what recently occurred, whether it is a conversation, a phone call, her pills or names and events. Yet she remembers events in the past and enjoys telling these stories as if in the telling she can touch those people and emotions. I found myself saying, "She is not the person she used to be." as I struggled to alter the reality to fit what had been. It takes great effort to impose a false reality onto the truth. I found that in doing so I was compromising the ability to be with who she is now and enjoy her just as she is. When I let go of being with who I hoped she could be I was able to enjoy her in the now, without the sorrow I had been feeling over what I perceived was the loss of the person she was.

Paradoxically, I consider she is the one completely present in the moment. It is I who am out of step, holding onto the past and frightened of the future. I would scream and cry claiming aloud to God, "You can't have her, I won't let her go! There must be a way to stop this!" wanting so much to hold on to my idea of who she should be or has been.

Stepping back, I see the greater the attachment the greater the pain. Could it be that Mina (my mother) in her soul's wisdom is helping me to adjust and that this thing called dementia is a way of easing into a final letting go? From the time I was born, hasn't it been a process of letting go of her?

First leaving the womb as a newborn. Then going to the first day of school - crying as she walked away. (I was unaware that she too was crying.) Years later going to college, excited by being on my own for the first time, followed by bouts of freshman homesickness. Even when I married, that was a reframing of our relationship and interdependency.

I find myself at a new threshold with her, afraid to open the next door. Can I support her as she enters her twilight, a silence and peace that she has explicitly told me she welcomes? Is it a matter of her surrendering to the cycle of life and death with grace, or is it is my acknowledgement that a life has been well-lived, that the whole of life is not dependent so much on the duration of life but rather on the whole-heartedness in which one enters each moment? And that indeed, there is nothing to let go of. Could it be that the door we all must open and pass through is a returning to home, an evaporation of temporal form into universal energy, and a joyous reunion? Could it be that the bodies we inhabit are not who we are, the houses we live in are all temporary attachments and that the connection I have with her and with all is much deeper, invisible yet felt, much more perennial than my suffering mind acknowledges? Who or what do I believe she really is such that I would ever lose her?

Could this be the most important lesson I will learn from my mother? To acknowledge the moment, to live fully in this instant, engaging in my life moment to moment, compassionately observing what is right there in front of me, opening myself to sorrow as much as to joy, to discomfort as equally as ease? As my mother taught me so long ago, ("*ver con los ojos del recien nacido*" – to see with the eyes of a newborn) am I able to come to my life and see the "beingness" of what is there without imposing the judgments, the perceptions, the categorizations my mind has constructed, that cause me pain and suffering? Can I see with the eyes of the newborn and in that way be present to her, honor and love her, right here, right now and stop fighting what is?

Isn't the greatest gift I can give her the gift of presence and acceptance and unconditional love? Aren't these the lessons she herself taught me? Can I stop fighting with what is and instead accept whatever process is occurring in the here and now?

We have a culture that describes life's passages in diagnostic terms. In a retreat I facilitated for Hospice of the Chesapeake the group articulated one of the guiding principles as "living-focused dying"; meaning moving away from the denial of death and engaging with the death process with great compassion and acceptance. And it is in that place of acceptance, that regardless of the circumstances, we may all be healed, even as we die.

Mina may not be physically dying, but this thing called

dementia is to my mind, a loss, robbing me of the relationship we have had. But it's not true. What is here and will always be here will be a deep connection to her being in whatever form it takes. My connection is a heart connection and the truth is, it doesn't require as much as my mind requires.

When next I see her, I will laugh at the funny stories she tells me, over and over again, about her life. I will share a glass of wine with her over a meal we cook together. I will let her know that its ok for her to be in whatever moment she is in, and that forever, I will be happy to be in that moment with her, and as an extension with anyone.

And that capacity to be fully present, living in the perfect moment, for me, may be the greatest lesson I ever learn from her.

Chapter Three
Beliefs and Reflections

"All serious daring starts from within."
~Eudora Welty

Three Shift Elements

hy is it that the things you say you really want seem just out of reach? You may beat yourself up about this, saying things like, "Well, if I really wanted it, I would just do it." Or "What is wrong with me that I cannot do this." Or "I must not be disciplined enough."

Maybe it is just really hard for you to do that one thing which you say you want to do. Maybe you fundamentally believe there really will be a "someday". Maybe you rationalize that it really wouldn't make a difference anyway. Maybe it is all of the above.

On a recent ride back from a workshop with a friend and colleague, we discussed our personal "Achilles heel". We heard ourselves saying similar things about what gets in our way as our clients. I had begun to formulate a hypothesis while in the workshop and this conversation eventually helped me better understand the difficulty you may encounter in making something happen.

I believe there are three major elements to shifting in a way that actually brings about the results you seek. First, there is a shift in perspective. You may be holding assumptions or simply not seeing something as possible or available. You make excuses for why you cannot possibly have or do something. There is a point where if you come to believe in the possibility of something, you shift into a place that what you need or want seems as essential as breathing. You begin to actually feel in your body, mind and emotional fields that in order for you to attain the quality of life you desire, that this dream, goal or vision is integral, and that it indeed supports other major components in your life. It moves from being something you have to do as a chore to being something you want to do in order to be fully alive. You no longer engage in excuses about how difficult it is to do or what might keep you from doing it. You just do it.

Which leads me to the second shift element: behavior. You begin to behave as if you are that person that you want to be. The shift in perspective allows you to create a new blueprint. You begin to live within the blueprint according to your behaviors and actions. If you want to be a writer, you start incorporating elements of a writing life. If you want to run a marathon, you start training. This does two things. It creates momentum by building onto your first shift in perspective. And it begins to re-create your reality around the goal or vision. It is real and accessible because you are doing it. And all the things that you said would hold you back disappear in the face of this new reality. You begin to organize your thoughts, behaviors and actions around this new reality. And that brings me to the third element, adding to your ability to sustain the results.

The third shift element is language. Your language begins to affirm your new perspective in both subtle and overt ways. Don't be lazy about language; use distinctions instead of generalizations. In manifesting a new shift, and through language, distinctions make the picture of what you are creating more lucid for you. And that clarity helps you distinguish your choices and decisions. You choose for your goals, for yourself without guilt or apology. It just is that way, not like an idea but firmly like a way of life. Your language moves from being tentative to affirmative. Your language also becomes more positive and optimistic. It "sustains" you even during the times that you – inevitably – meet with obstacles and difficulties. It cements your resolve in a tangible manner.

To further your ability to create these shifts in your life, or to move through your transitions, you also need to enlist support from others. This supportive community becomes

Alicia Rodriguez

the bridge between all the elements. You must be choosy about your support. Determine first, what kind of specific support is needed. Will it be professional support, such as a personal trainer, or an instructor, a personal coach or an educational venue? What support can you get in holistic terms? How can you be supported, mentally (learning, reading), physically (good eating, sleeping, exercise), spiritually (time for reflection, yoga) and emotionally (your partners, friends)?

After determining specifically what you need, you make direct and specific requests to garner that support.

Periodically, you re-evaluate and adjust. Your environments are ever changing and the need to be fluid is essential to long-term success. Do not be surprised if while evaluating, you discover another shift beginning. This is the path of personal evolution, and although you look for sustainable results, remember that this is a dynamic process.

With self-awareness and support you will grow and develop personally and professionally. Your dreams will become more than possibilities, they will become reality. You will begin to recognize and use this three-part process of growth purposely: perspective, behavior and language.

Welcome to your evolving life!

*"The best and safest thing is to keep a balance in your life,
acknowledge the great powers around us and in us. If you can do
that, and live that way, you are really a wise man." (or woman!)*
~ Euripides

The Myth of Balance

Balance is a myth. There, I said it out loud.
To many a coach, this is heresy. But let me say it
again: there is no such thing as achieving
balance in your life. It cannot be done.

Balance, as we tend to use the word, is a concept constructed as an ideal in theory, but as a self-defeating goal in reality. You feel disempowered because the standard you hold of what it means to be in balance is unattainable. You are defeated before you begin. This is especially true for women who are culturally set up to fail by a society that demands perfect mothers, wives, executives, soccer moms, business owners and human beings – all at once.

What do you have instead of balance? You have choice. You can make choices that will either positively or negatively affect you. Or you cannot make a choice, and that in itself becomes the choice.

Have you ever watched a gemologist weighing a jewel on a scale? On one side she places a weight and on the other she places the jewel(s). The balance shifts from side to side, depending on what is placed upon the scale. When something is removed from the jewel side, the weight becomes the heavier side. When more jewels are added it shifts the weight to the jewel side. This is what occurs for all of you, given any day, even any one moment.

There are times when you may be required to meet deadlines, or you must do more than normal to meet someone else's needs. We may have set a career goal for yourself that requires more time and dedication. Perhaps your desire to own or grow a successful company means putting other parts of yourself on hold. You choose. You shift the weight from one area to the other. It is usually for a limited amount of time. The cause of this imbalance (which is really a choice) is resolved or removed and you can shift your attention back to yourself or to other areas in your life. Over the course of a day, month or year, this balancing act moves from one side to the other, depending on what is required of you and how you choose.

What you control are the options placed on the scale, how long it remains, and at what point it is removed. Although at any given moment you may not "be in balance", over the course of time your conscious choices can provide the ability to shift your attention and energy as needed. You cease to tolerate what doesn't serve you.

The idea is to set boundaries around what you will or will not add to your side of the scale. And you determine those boundaries based on what you value. At any point there may be a need to adjust within your immediate requirements with the intention of resolving it and bringing yourself back into balance.

A re-definition of your ideal of balance is called for. Balance needs to be re-defined in the larger context of your life. Life happens and there are times where you are required to give more than you normally would give. But if you choose with self-awareness and consider your well being and longer-term goals, you can remain both healthy and productive.

Balance, as defined by our ideology, is myth. Choice is real.

The Hologram Paradox

*I*n a coaching session with a client, she was speaking about boundaries. Her assertion was that boundaries did not exist because we are all one. She chose not to separate herself but to remain as one with all that is.

I asked her to consider that she was moving into an "either/or" situation. Either I have boundaries or I am one with all. What if you could have boundaries that maintained your personal integrity (in the sense of wholeness) and still remain one with all that there is? I asked. Could you then accept that you can make statements and create actions to support your personal wholeness while remaining connected?

The example I gave her was the Hologram. Indeed, the hologram is a paradox or what I consider a "koan"- a riddle that cannot be answered with the mind. I asked her to meditate on the question, "How can I be connected with all while being singularly whole at the same time?" This is the Hologram Paradox.

The word hologram is derived from the Greek words, holo, meaning whole, and gram, meaning message. Therefore, hologram means whole message.

The hologram is based upon Nobel Prize winner Dennis Gabor's theory concerning interference patterns. Gabor theorized in 1947 that each crest of the wave pattern contains the whole information of its original source, and that this information could be stored on film and reproduced. This is why it is called a hologram.

A pebble, dropped in a still pond, is the most basic example used to describe the wave interference process. If you drop a pebble into a pond, it creates an infinitely expanding circular wave pattern. If you drop two pebbles into a pond the waves' crests would eventually meet. The intersecting points of the waves' crests are called the points of interference. The interference of two or more waves will carry the whole information about all the waves.

Another application for the hologram is found in the work of David Bohm. Bohm (1917-1992) was one of the most distinguished theoretical physicists of his generation. Underlying his innovative approach to many different issues was the fundamental idea that beyond the visible, tangible world there lies a deeper, intricate order of undivided wholeness.

David Bohm's unique insights about quantum physics led to the suggestion that what appears in an explicit sense as separate particles, as an external, independent world, is ultimately linked. "I am in the world, and the world is in me." Bohm called this way of seeing things the "holographic paradigm" – suggesting that the whole of the world is enfolded within our awareness, in fact within every aspect of the world. This is the basis of the work done in the practice of dialogue, a formal way of conversing that taps into the collective wisdom of a group.

Our world is undergoing trying times. There is war, the economy is uncertain, and many individuals are experiencing breakdown – and breakthrough. My question to you is this. How do you relate your own experience to the larger experience of the human race? How do you relate the experience of the human race to your own experience? Can you see yourself as the pebble in the pond while seeing yourself as the pond itself? Can you be whole, unique and separate person while being integrated and connected into the larger whole of humanity? What is possible for you out of this inquiry? What do you then see that you could not see before?

Like koans, these difficult questions require quiet reflection and an open mind, heart and imagination. You may gain a different perspective on your situation. You may find you are not as alone as you believed you were. You may find kinship with those you may never even meet. Much is possible from reflecting on these questions. I encourage you to do so, from wherever you are, from whatever point of view you hold.

Who knows what ripples you may cast into the stillness of the pond.

Alicia Rodriguez

"I say, if it's going to be done, let's do it. Let's not put it in the hands of fate. Let's not put it in the hands of someone who doesn't know me. I know me best. Then take a breath and go ahead."
~Anita Baker

At Cause or At Choice?

*I*t's Monday morning. The alarm rings. Do you wake up excited to start a new day? Or do you envision your day, and your week, as an onslaught of stress, negativity, or perhaps are you overwhelmed?

Millions of people enter their weeks in this manner. Many people "sleep" through a large portion of their lives. This "sleep" has to do with comfort and fear and all sorts of emotions and patterns.

Do you live "at cause"? By that I mean do you feel you are at the mercy of the events in your life or you are simply not living on purpose, merely following the path of least resistance? Are you the person who takes a job because someone told you it was available and the money was good? Or do you remain in an unfulfilling marriage because it seems like a comfortable habit, never mind that you no longer speak or share dreams together? Or are you the young person who goes to medical school to become a doctor because your father or mother is a doctor? There is no real choosing here. Events or outside influences direct the course of your life, bouncing you from job to job, place to place, and relationship to relationship.

What would it be like to live "at choice"? What would it be like to actually look inside to determine what really matters then actively and purposely design your life or work around those things that really matter to you now? Can you imagine interviewing for a job you knew met your personal criteria, a job that you knew you could excel in for an organization you could contribute to and where you would be acknowledged and rewarded? How much more positive would this experience be for you? Would you feel more powerful in this interview knowing you were choosing as much as they were?

Take time to evaluate carefully how you want to live the rest of your life. What do you want to take with you and leave behind for this journey? Choose with intention and purpose. The decision is the right decision if you are making it according to your own authentic personal values.

What gets in the way of being "at choice"?

• **Habits:** These are behaviors we have integrated into a routine so much so that we don't realize we do them. We are conditioned to respond over and over again in a particular way and our responses become thought-less.

• **Fear:** The what if fear, the but, but fear, the I am not enough fear, the what will I lose fear, the I might actually get what I want fear, the I will be a whole person fear, the what will they think fear, and on and on.

• **Unavoidable circumstances:** An example: you have a health issue that requires attention. Within these circumstances, what can you do to eventually reach your aspirations, whether within the same venue or in another arena that still provides satisfaction? You can choose to work with the circumstances or you can remain at cause and fill your life with resentment.

• **It's not my fault:** Whose fault would it be if not yours? Ask yourself: what role am I playing here in this dynamic that keeps me from my desired outcome? Eventually you will see that you actually do play a role in your life and your circumstances and in every interaction in your life. Once you see that you are part of the dynamic, you can begin to choose on purpose and take responsibility for your outcomes.

• **Silent beliefs:** These are things you believe about yourself that usually start with "I am", "I am not", "I can't", "I couldn't" and the like. Some examples I have heard are: "I can't do math" or "I am not smart enough, thin enough, good enough", etc. These beliefs may have been handed down to you or you may believe them because of a past event. They are so ingrained in you that you can't see that they drive your behaviors and your inaction around your life.

Power lies in your freedom to choose the path of your life. Happiness comes from choosing the life you really want. Peace comes from fully living that life aligned with what really matters to you.

How will you live your life today? At cause? Or at choice? It really is up to you.

*"...Until one is committed there is hesitancy, the chance to
draw back, always ineffectiveness. Concerning all acts of
initiative (and creation), there is one elementary truth,
the ignorance of which kills countless ideas and splendid
plans: that the moment one definitely commits oneself,
then Providence moves too. All sorts of things occur
to help one that would never otherwise have occurred.
A whole stream of events issues from the decision,
raising in one's favor all manner of unforeseen incidents
and meetings and material assistance, which no man
could have dreamed would have come his way.
I have learned a deep respect for one of Goethe's couplets:
Whatever you can do, or dream you can, begin it.
Boldness has genius, power and magic in it.
Begin it now!"*
~W.H. Murray

Commitment

*T*he word "commitment" seems to be thrown
around quite a bit. Have you considered what
"commitment" means to you?

The Merriam-Webster's Collegiate Dictionary defines
commitment as "an agreement or pledge to do something in
the future; ... the state or an instance of being obligated or
emotionally impelled (a commitment to a cause)." To me, the
word commitment denotes more than a promise to do or not
do something. There is a high level of emotional investment
and soul-centered passion in making a commitment or having a commitment to something. Without that passionate element, the action or cause may become more of a "should" or
obligation rather than a vision that draws you powerfully
forward. That passion enables you to move through the
inevitable obstacles you encounter in manifesting the dream
or vision that forms the foundation of your commitment.

You connect to others through your commitments.
When you commit to being at service of others, for example,

you connect to your mutual humanity and the enhancement of the quality of your life and others lives. When you commit to the environment, you are making a deep connection to nature and to living in that connection as a supporting element in the web of life. When you commit to education, you connect to children and adult learners and teachers, and as such you connect to yourself as teacher or student. When you commit to human rights, you demand for yourself the respect that you seek to ensure for others.

Commitment supersedes contracts, legal agreements, and other constructs meant to enforce promises. Commitment cannot be regulated. True commitment sources from within, and the contract is merely the outward manifestation of what is true for us internally. True commitment is deeper than contracts. It has more to do with who you are rather than what you do.

What you commit to reflects who you are at your deepest level. Being deeply committed to someone or something reflects what really matters to you. It is action driven from your essential self that propels you in a particular direction. It is the soul voiced aloud.

Commitment can be frightening. It often asks more of you than you may believe you are capable of. Yet, intuitively, you enter uncharted territory knowing somewhere inside of yourself that in making a commitment you begin to realize your dreams. Amazingly, the universe moves in mysterious ways to bring you what you need in order to engage in your new adventure.

There is another side of commitment. What happens when you have fulfilled your commitment and it is time to move on? Or when that which you were committed to has ceased to hold the passion and emotional investment for you and indeed, may be in the way of your own further development? What is the cost of commitments over-extended? How do you honorably move on?

This often happens in relationships and changes in

careers or jobs. When things in your life change, or when you grow apart because the passion behind your commitment is no longer present and cannot be resurrected, explore your next steps. I am often asked about how to make this transition. Inherent in the question is the rest of the question: How do I make this transition—without hurting anyone? I do not know if these transitions can be made without hurting anyone. The question is less about "if" one moves away from a previous commitment; it's more "how" to move toward a new commitment that reflects your evolutionary process. When the dynamics of connections are changed so that expectations are not being met, someone may feel abandoned or hurt. These questions are important to ask.

Are you being honest about your change in commitment?

Do you feel you are leaving the relationship with integrity?

Are you putting into place or keeping in place fundamental commitments (such as care of the children, referring the client to another professional, helping others to adjust by communicating or by putting other structures in place)?

Does your new commitment align with who you are and your potential and the values you hold? Or are you moving away from what matters most to you out of fear?

Are you open to listening to the pain or discomfort of those you leave behind (without needing to "solve" anything) as they may want or need to be heard?

Is this a healthy and positive move for you?

With every step you take in your personal development you move closer to one thing and further away from something else. You needn't judge this. It is as natural as the changing of the seasons. You have your own seasons and cycles. And with those seasonal changes come new commitments and the dissolution of others. Be intentional about what is important and you will find that you will know when it is time to move on.

"Listen. Make a way for yourself inside yourself.
Stop looking in the other way of looking."
~Jelaluddin Rumi

Let the Bonsai Be the Bonsai

I am continually reminded how lucky I am to be a coach and to have the clients I have. I learn from my clients and it is always extraordinary when they share their learning with me. One client, a creative, expressive, thoughtful young woman, mom and singer/songwriter shared with me her "11 Things I Know Now That I Didn't Know I Knew Before." You may recognize some of these in yourself as well.

1. Let the bonsai be the bonsai. (For those of you who don't know, the best care of a bonsai is not to DO things to it, but instead to allow it to form itself and care for it in ways that support its own growth on its own terms.)

2. I can get in my own way by trying too hard, i.e., less effort can produce greater results.

3. It's not all or nothing. I don't have to do everything. I just have to do something.

4. Don't focus on not failing. Focus on succeeding.

5. I need a support group/community to act within.

6. Being present in this moment is all that's required.

7. By making the time to do what I want- what is best for me- I still have the time to do the things

I "have to" do and I do them in a more positive and effective way.

8. It's OK to give myself permission.

9. The journey is as enjoyable as the destination.

10. I might as well just go ahead and get started.

11. What I do and what I want to do is good, nurturing and life giving. I owe it to myself, to my family and to the world to create because no one can do exactly what I can do.

Ask yourself which of these 11 insights apply to you too! (In gratitude to Regina V.)

*"This kind of forgetting does not erase memory, it lays
the emotion surrounding the memory to rest."*
~ Clarissa Pinkola Estes

Up Until Now...

I think a lot about "stories". Stories help us probe in places that our minds cannot reach. Stories evoke feelings, emotions, ideas, insights, dreams and more. Stories are powerful.

Do you have a personal narrative or story? What is the story you tell yourself about who you are? Is that story keeping you from moving forward in your life? Did someone tell you a story "once upon a time" that you began to own as your own, even though you did not write the story? What does that story say about you and who you are? Does it tell you who you are capable of being? Or does it keep you tied to a past that no longer applies to the way you want to live your life?

My job is to listen for my clients' stories. It is a privilege to witness another person's story. It is drama, comedy, mystery and more all tied up in this one human being. I will often ask the client, what part of this story is really you? What part do you believe so much that it defines you in limiting ways? And then I ask my clients to begin using the words, "Up until now…"

One client claims that she has never been a social person and that networking has always been difficult. Yet, as an entrepreneur, she recognizes the need to network to build her visibility. I challenge her to use the words, "Up until now – I have not been comfortable networking." And I add, "From this point forward…" and together we begin to write a new story for her. In her case, "from this point forward, I will have one-to-one conversations with people who I find interesting or whom I share something in common with." She tells me, "Well, I can do that!" And she begins to gradually ease into her new, more expansive, story.

What is the story you tell yourself? Fill in the blank, "Up until now, I (have not, could not, did not, was, was not, etc.)

Then add, "From this point forward, I (can, will, etc.)

You can choose your story! Which story would you prefer - a story of limitations and defeat? Or would you rather tell yourself an empowering story, a bold adventure story, a story of victory? You are the only one choosing the story!

Special thanks to Neil Stroul, faculty member and executive coach, Georgetown University Leadership Program, for helping me discover a new personal story. Also, special thanks to Pat Lynch, my mentor and friend, who showed me long ago that I was capable of a bigger story!

*"Two monks were once traveling together down a muddy road.
A heavy rain was falling. Coming around the bend, they met
a lovely girl in a silk kimono and sash, unable to cross
the intersection. "Come on, girl," said the first monk.
Lifting her in his arms, he carried her over the mud.
The second monk did not speak again until that night
when they reached a lodging temple. Then he no longer
could restrain himself. "We monks do not go near females,"
he said. "It is dangerous. Why did you do that?"
"I left the girl there," the first monk said.
"Are you still carrying her?"
~ A Zen Story*

What You Still Carry

What story will you tell me when you sit with me? Will I hear you tell me a story about hurt and disappointment or betrayal of trust? Will I hear self-blame between the lines? Will your body betray your words as you shrink into the soft leather chair as you tell me the story of your life in the soft light of my office?

Stories remain with us long after the initial event occurs. Some of these stories are alive in a person's mind, body and spirit. You can hear it in the tone or see it in the body. The story becomes a heavy burden on the individual telling the story.

In repeating a story, it becomes more cemented; as if repeating it would validate the emotions or vindicate the storyteller in some way. The story is "nurtured" and continues to live as truth through its telling. It reinforces itself.

What if the story were to be altered a bit? There is great power in telling your story; there is healing, sharing and connection in storytelling. But when the story has you (as my friend Neil says) then you no longer have the power to create your new, more positive, more empowering, story.

What if the story were told as "that was then" and you added, "and this is now"? What if you didn't tell your story as if the past would determine your future? What if you were to choose consciously which stories bear repeating and reinforcing and which stories are only one element in your whole experience, not overshadowing other elements or your future?

What is the story you are telling yourself over and over again? What is the story that has you? How does it feel in your body when you tell the story? How does it feel in your heart when you tell the story? What might be an alternative to this story? What do you need to do to heal from the story you tell? How can you gently release the story? And what is the new story you want to create and live? What do you still carry that is best left in the past? Isn't it time to put down your burden? Write a new story, that is healing and self-affirming. Your past need not dictate your future. There are still many, many stories to write!

"Often people attempt to live their lives backwards: they try to have more things, or more money, in order to do more of what they want so that they will be happier. The way it actually works is the reverse. You must first be who you really are, then, do what you need to do, in order to have what you want."
~Margaret Young

Life is a Choice

Each and every day, indeed each and every minute, you are faced with choices. Sometimes, you may not be aware that there is a choice to make.

When you get up in the morning, you can choose to have a positive outlook or a negative outlook. You may not think about this as you are brushing your teeth, but you can choose to begin your day one way or the other. It is not so much about what is happening around you but more it is about what is happening within you that makes a difference in how your day progresses.

You know that at any given moment you must choose one thing over another to achieve a goal or outcome, but too often you have not set up our life's framework to support making a choice that is aligned with your values and sustains your well being. These are the times that you can feel unempowered to make a choice that you wish you could make. I often hear people say, "I really don't have a choice." The truth is that you may not like the consequences associated with any of the choices available to you, not that there is no choice.

So what needs to be present to really live your life as a choice? There are key elements that must be present for you to be master of your destiny in a world where you may have very little actual control.

- **Define what matters most to you.** Without knowing what is really important to you, it will be impossible to make a choice that is aligned with the way you envision your life. Good choices cannot be made in a vacuum, without comparing them to a standard of measurement that I call personal vision - a picture of what your ideal life wants to be.

- **Create a structure that supports getting what you need and want with minimal struggle and fear.** You are apt to make choices driven by fear instead of making choices directed by desire, passion and growth if you haven't planned to have what you want in your life. As an example, when faced with a job evaluation, you can entertain thoughts such as "I should be grateful to have a job, to get any raise at all", when in reality you have performed beyond the standards and deserve to ask for and receive a raise or some other compensation. But you don't negotiate out of fear that you may be left with less or nothing. Consider some options – you can remain in a job that drains you or that you resent, adapt the present job, or move to another job that is meaningful and rewarding? At some point, the balance will shift; why wait until there is so much pain that you cannot plan to be successful any longer?

- **Anticipate those things that matter to you and *plan* to have them in your life.** If you really want to retire at 40, create a plan, a life framework that supports that goal. If you know you want to have children and want to continue on your career path, what actions need to be taken now to bring this about later. Not creating a plan is like not making a decision. A non-plan, like a non-decision, is a decision in itself, a decision of non-choice.

• **You can't have it all, all the time.** The concept of having it all, all the time is a set up for exhaustion and sabotages you. Sheryl Crow in her album, "Soaking Up the Sun", sings, "It's not having what you want, it's wanting what you have." I love that line! There is peace in accepting and engaging from exactly where you are and indeed, it is the only way to know what steps may be next on our journey.

• **Understand the distinction between choice and decision.** A decision has to do with two options. A choice includes multiple options. When faced with a decision, ask yourself if there are not other options you may not have considered. For example, you like your job and the company but you don't like the work. The decision may limit you to staying or leaving. Including options such as staying and moving to another department or adjusting your job responsibilities or asking for flexible hours are all options that can be explored before resorting to either/or decisions. But here again, you must know what it is that matters most to you in order to negotiate, ask for and plan for a meaningful assignment.

• **You are not responsible for the responses of others to your choices.** Everyone has an opinion on how you choose. You are not responsible for their point of view, or their response to your choices. They may be affected, but the purpose is not to change others, but to align your choices with how you want your life to be. There is only one way to fail, and that is to try to please everyone.

• **Add "and" to your vocabulary.** The use of the word "and" instead of "or" will open up other options to you. A very simple, but effective, shift. Practice saying and instead of or.

• **Habits and cycles keep us from choice.** You have a lifetime of developing habits and getting caught up in negative cycles. When you become self aware you notice these habits. Break old, ineffective habits. Determine what you need to do, or undo, to break cycles. If you have been overworking to keep up with projects, and you are tired and begin to make mistakes, then is working late hours actually effective and helpful to you or your clients? Do the opposite, get out of work at a reasonable hour, spend time with your family or on things you enjoy, and get rest so when you are working you are most effective. Break the workaholic cycle.

• **Know that your choices will change.** As your life evolves and includes other life events, what matters to you may change and so will your choices. The key is to be aware that who you are today and what you need today may not be the same as yesterday. Choose for today, not for yesterday, not for tomorrow. There are only a few decisions that impact your whole life. Keep this perspective when you make your choices and decisions. To make it easier begin by saying, "for now...I will..." It is just for now.

• **There can be limited choices.** There are times of extreme stress, such as unemployment for long periods of time, divorce and single parenthood or financial catastrophes that will limit one's options. You may find it necessary to make choices out of the fundamental need to survive. Don't judge the choices made out of survival needs against choices made when the environment is more flexible. If you have been out of work for a long period and have a family to support, you may have to take any job to provide income until times are better. Remember, these times are usually temporary and these decisions are not permanent. Times of stress illustrate the importance of creating a supportive life framework early in your life to assist in challenging times.

Even in times of great stress, even in times where you are feeling powerless, the knowledge that you can still choose how you respond can give you strength and courage. Apply this courage to create strategies in your daily life, so you will come to experience Life as a Choice.

"Every now and then go away, have a little relaxation, for when you come back to your work your judgment will be surer. Go some distance away because then the work appears smaller and more of it can be taken in at a glance and a lack of harmony and proportion is more readily seen."
~Leonardo Da Vinci

Seek Harmony Not Balance

Our lives are complex and unpredictable. Especially for women, balance creates an "either/or" dynamic which translates for women: damned if you do/damned if you don't. For example, you can work out and take care of yourself or you can do the grocery shopping, or the report that is due; you can go to work and have a career, or you can become a stay-at-home-mom, etc. Because of women's multiple roles, and the lack of support for these in our culture, the myth of balance imposes double bind situations and unrealistic expectations. Women can criticize themselves over not being able to do or have it all. This applies to men as well, who have their own set of cultural expectations that leaves little time or sometimes permission for self-care, following a passion or going to their kids' games and activities.

Harmony is different, however. I think of Mother Nature and the harmony that is created, even out of chaos. Think about weather patterns in nature or the ebb and flow of the tides. Nature's harmony takes into account the whole system, not merely one or two aspects of a system.

When you affect or influence one area of your life, inevitably other areas are also affected. As an example, if you are hired for a new job, you may have to allow more time for commuting which means you may have to move your day-care from one town to another, which means you may need to allow more money to pay for that daycare, and on and on. One change will affect multiple areas of your life.

Balance is a duality. Harmony is integral and whole. You are either in or out of balance. Harmony seeks a synergy of multiple parts of the whole that allows flexibility, expansion and contraction, perhaps all at the same time in order to keep the entity, person or organization fluid, healthy and thriving.

Harmony allows for more choices and more areas to balance out; not just two areas. If you consistently think in terms of maintaining harmony, instead of balance, you will have additional reserves of energy, time, money or resources for those times when you meet with the unexpected. You have more options for being successful. Harmony allows for more flexibility as it increases your awareness of your environment.

Consider nature as your teacher. Next time there is a storm, watch the natural elements. Notice how all the elements interact and shift in response to the storm. Your life, whether sunny or stormy, is similar and seeking harmony will help you lead a life with more flow and ease.

Accept the Unacceptable

She arrived completely stressed, talking a mile a minute and fidgeting in her chair. "I can't bear the thought of going home for the holidays. My mother will immediately ask me if I have enough money to dress better; then she will go into the litany of how 'art' is not a 'real job' and how I should've been a doctor like my sister. I wish she would just welcome me for once just like I am and stop with the remarks."

He arrived angry and frustrated, foregoing all pleasantries and launched into his story. "My boss is a jerk. Every time I try to show some initiative, he picks apart my work. Review time is coming up and I am sure it won't be good. He is so picky and refuses to see the big picture. I don't know how I can handle this except to leave."

Do these stories sound familiar? Perhaps you have been in a similar situation or have heard others complain of like situations. Your first impulse in situations like these may be to force a change in the other person or the environment. You don't want to accept the situation is what it is. In refuting the current reality, you will not see options that may be open to you. Inevitably you concentrate on the elements outside of yourself – on the other person, on the organization or on the environment. Your energy is spent on trying to change those things that you do not control or cannot control. This expenditure of energy will inevitably wear you down.

Let's take a look at each story. In the first story, the client is dealing with her familial relationship and projecting into the future what the reality will be based on her past experience of her visits home. When I asked her how long this type of conversation has occurred she said "forever". I asked her what it was about the situation that most bothered her. She replied, "Why can't my mom just accept me the way I am?" My next question to her was "Why can't you just accept the way your mom is?" It never occurred to her that she might be the one not accepting of her mother. I could see the "aha" on her face. "Gosh, I am doing the same thing to her!" I asked, "What would happen if you accepted your mom just the way she is? How might things be different?" She realized that if she were to accept her mother as she was, what she had previously experienced as criticism would be transformed to concern. And that concern was something she could address in a centered manner. She would no longer feel the need to fight or debate. As it turned out, the next time she went home, she and her mother enjoyed each other for the first time in years.

In the second story, I asked the client to tell me what he felt was unacceptable about the situation. He said that picking apart his work was unacceptable. I asked, "What if you accepted that your boss might be right and that your work was not done correctly?" He paused and considered this. It turned out that he felt that he did not fully understand the objectives of the department and that there were times he would do his work to justify his time. He concluded that there was indeed an incomplete or unaddressed conversation between he and his boss. He later approached his boss with a well-articulated request to clarify the department's objectives and the standards of measurement for his position. This initiated a larger meeting and curiously others came forth expressing the same confusion. His ability to consider what he had previously felt was unacceptable, contributed to an open conversation at work.

Consider when or where in your life you are feeling stress from a situation that you feel is not what you want it to be. Ask yourself what about this is unacceptable. Then ask yourself what would happen if you could accept this situation. How might the situation then be different and what possibilities or outcomes might arise from this shift in perspective? There are always things that are truly unacceptable, but if you begin by asking this question, you may find that accepting the present situation is the first real step in transforming it.

"Live with intention. Walk to the edge. Listen hard. Practice wellness. Play with abandon. Laugh. Choose with no regret. Appreciate your friends. Continue to learn. Do what you love. Live as this is all there is. "
~Mary Anne Radmacher

A Lesson in Intention

*T*here is a story from the medieval Christian tradition that gives me pause to consider how I enter into my day and my work. A traveler came upon a worksite and saw two men carrying large stones. One man was working wearily with a sullen expression on his face, while the other man was cheerfully singing as he busily carried stone after stone. "What are you doing?" asked the traveler of the sullen worker. "Laying stone" was his reply. "What are you doing?" asked the traveler addressing the man singing cheerfully. "Building a cathedral" was his reply.

Every day you can choose if you will start your day as the bricklayer or the builder of cathedrals. Every day you can look in the mirror and choose your own greatness or choose to be the victim of circumstances. Based on that choice, you will experience your day accordingly.

This is the role of intention. Intention is the first step in reaching your potential. Your intention focuses you on the correct actions and behaviors that will produce a desired outcome. And your intention will either inspire you or create struggle, much like the illustration of the different perspectives of the workers in the story.

Intention is the foundation and action is the driver that moves our intention into reality. If you see yourself as a partner in your firm, then you will behave as one. If you see myself as a caring parent (or son or daughter), you will behave with care and affection. If you see yourself as unimportant, then you will behave as if your actions do not matter.

One client repeatedly had disastrous relationships, yet what he desired most was to have a long-term, caring relationship. When I asked him what the most important criteria in choosing who he dated was, he said, "I don't want to make the same mistakes I made before." His intention is to avoid a painful situation. I pointed out that there might be a more useful and appropriate intention. "What would it be like if instead of avoiding disaster, you intended to create a loving, long-lived relationship? What would you do differently?" His energy was being negatively channeled into avoiding something painful instead of positively channeled into creating something wonderful. When confronted with this alternative intention he realized that his fear of dating and his sense of self-worth were based on avoidance. Changing his intention, he entered into new relationships with much more joy, curiosity and enjoyment. And of course, joy, curiosity and enjoyment are attractive! His results showed up in better relationships as he embarked on finding a life partner.

Ask yourself, are you busy avoiding problems or would you prefer to create possibilities? The energy associated with doing one as opposed to the other is vastly different. Which would you prefer? You choose.... and you choose each and every day you look in that mirror...

*Tether: a rope or chain attached to something at the other end,
thus restricting movement*

Tethers

*E*very October in Albuquerque, New Mexico the Hot
Air Balloon Festival takes place with hundreds of
giant, colorful globes launching into the sky. I have
seen pictures of this event taken by friends of mine who have
attended. Huge, colorful balloons lift gracefully into the air,
their lines untethered defying gravity. What amazes me is
that these extremely large balloons filled with gas could be
restrained from flying off by tethers or ropes attached to the
ground. I realize these are strong and rather thick ropes, yet
when I see the size of the balloons I still wonder about how
the rope is strong enough to be an appropriate restraint for
something whose natural state is airborne.

Why my fascination with hot air balloons and tethers? A
metaphor occurred to me. I can imagine all of us being like
the fully realized balloon whose natural state is to fly. Once
you wake up to your life there is a drive to launch into your
potential, into the life you are drawn to live. Yet you wait.
You wait until you have more money, until the kids are
grown, until you retire, until…whatever. You tell yourself, "I
can't do that because I am not smart enough, rich enough,
pretty enough, successful enough, etc. etc. Yet here you sit,
with a desire to launch into your full life, tethered to your
past or to your current state, unable to release the tethers that
bind you. Why do you do this?

You do this because you actually believe a couple
of things.

• You believe that, although your natural state may
be to "fly", or in Maslow's language, to self-actualize,
you see yourself limited by the stories you tell yourself. These I will call tethers.

- You believe that these tethers are much stronger than they may actually be; that you have no or limited power to release the tethers about who you are, what you have to offer and the possibilities that are available to you.

- You are afraid. The tethers provide a sense of safety and security. You can hold onto something, You are attached to something. In releasing the tethers you risk uncertainty and not knowing. That void between where you are and where you want to be looks scary. You forget that the emptiness can be a blank canvas full of possibilities.

- If you release the tethers, you may lose control. The illusion is that you actually are in control yet the reality is that at any given moment your world will be turned upside down. You prefer the illusion of control to the uncertainty of something new.

- Adventure. You have forgotten how to be adventuresome, to be an explorer. Exploration into your personal life and what drives you requires courage and reflection and the time to be in a state of inquiry. Your complex life does not support this inquiry into self and what really matters to you, so you remain tethered, not purposefully entering into the adventure that is your life.

If you find yourself saying, "I would do X, if only..." recognize that what comes after the "if only" is probably a tether based on a story you have created that limits you. What would you do if you were five times bolder? Once you answer it, notice the tethers that keep you from living full out, from moving into the action that will realize your dreams and goals. Now ask yourself, "How can I release these tethers?" "What is the limiting belief behind this and how do I create a new belief or story that allows me to fly?"

Once you are airborne, you will find yourself so enthralled by the view that all your passion for life and your sense of self will surely be revealed and will support the journey. Revel in your life. Take flight.

Chapter Four
Work and Goals

"…you are the only person alive who has sole custody of your life.
Your particular life. Your entire life. Not just your life at a desk,
or your life on the bus, or in the car, or at the computer.
Not just the life of your mind, but the life of your heart.
Not just your bank account, but your soul."
~Anna Quindlen in
A Short Guide to A Happy Life

Possibility or Opportunity

*Y*ou are a candidate for promotion to a high level job. Your business is doubling in size as your client base expands. You are in a transition, not sure whether to remain in a corporate environment or jump into entrepreneurship.

These are typical dilemmas faced by many individuals. Indeed, possibilities, as welcome as they are, can be overwhelming. But how do you decide if that possibility is actually an opportunity? What makes the decision? What appears as an opportunity may well be best left as a possibility.

Possibilities are not opportunities. They are what is possible but the question is, "Is this the right choice for me?" If the answer is yes, then you are looking at an opportunity. But what is possible is not always what is optimal or best for you. There is a subtle gap between possibility and opportunity. What transcends that gap has to do with your "personal criteria", or your values, what really matters to you.

A software engineer is passionate about his technology and uses his creativity to design innovative programs. He is so proficient, he is promoted to manager at a higher salary. Most would congratulate him for his rise "up the ladder". In six months, he goes from an enthusiastic employee to an unmotivated, abrupt manager.

The possibility of promotion was not measured against his passion for technology and his independent work-style.

What he valued most was removed in his promotion. This was not an opportunity although it may have appeared as such because all of our "should's" were present: climbing the ladder, title, money. Through coaching he articulated his dissatisfaction with his management position and proposed an alternative possibility. This led to a return to the technical aspects of the job but moving into more complex, higher level software programming. He retained a portion of his raise. He was ecstatic!

A senior VP of a healthcare company is weary of trying to juggle work and family with no support from her company. Indeed, the company frowns on any time off despite her achievements and ability to produce beyond expectations. She is presented with possibilities: to stay at the same company and work out her situation – to partner with four others and a sponsor to create a new company – or to branch out on her own. How does she choose which is the true opportunity? When I ask her what initiated these conversations and she evaluates what really matters to her right now, she answers that it is the desire to be with her children with a flexible schedule and still have a career with meaning and income. But most important is the desire to have control over her life. That is her personal criteria and each possibility must be weighed against that criteria. She decides for the entrepreneurship despite the appearance of less security. She is relieved and excited. She chose to value her own inner criteria over the external pulls.

Possibility or Opportunity? You will only know the answer when you are crystal clear about what really matters to you. When you can give yourself permission to weigh your possibilities against your personal criteria *without judgment* you will discover your true opportunity. It may surprise you when you choose for what you really want or need over the strident, judgmental voice of your mind and the well-meaning advice of others. Only you know your personal criteria. Be true to yourself.

"Besides the noble art of getting things done, there is the noble art of leaving things undone. The wisdom of life consists in the elimination of nonessentials."
~Lin Yutang

Essentially You

ere is a challenge. Eliminate one thing this week that takes up your time and energy and does nothing to align with your truest nature. Did you feel that pang in your stomach, the "Oh, no, not that!" feeling? What is essential to your life? How much of your life is devoted to the non-essential, to the up-keep of a lifestyle that keeps you running the wheel like a hamster in its cage, going nowhere fast. The sight of a blank space in your calendar begs to be filled lest you declare yourself unproductive, or at worst, lazy. You complain about never having enough time while your cup runs over.

Consider that at least 40 percent of what is in your calendar is there to make you feel good about yourself. It proves that you are that high-achiever, the go-getter, the go-to person at the office or at home. Like cleaning out your closets, clean out your calendar and clean out your life. Remove the non-essentials by consciously asking yourself the reason you are saying yes to the commitments you make. As you eviscerate your calendar, new blank spaces light up your screen inviting you to fill them in again. Resist the urge!

Begin to consciously choose who you spend time with and what you spend your time doing. First, keep the essentials, those people and activities that support the way you choose to lead your life. These may include your health, your friends or family, hobbies or spiritual practice. Notice how these are exactly the things that place last in the race for time. Change the course of your day by placing these first and then assessing what you need or want to include after these. Non-essential activities drain you and often anchor you to a way of life that is void of passion and spirit.

Choose on purpose what you will keep and what you will eliminate. Notice those times when you are ill and are forced to be still or navigate your life with only the most elemental tools. Did the world fall apart? Were your clients still there? Did your children forget your name?

No, none of that happened.

So if your world doesn't fall apart in the worst of circumstances, why wait until then to learn what is essential and non-essential. Take some time now to clean out your life. In those blank spaces you will find quiet and the energy to flow with the life you really desire.

"D" is for Organized

I know of no one who can honestly say, "I am organized all of the time." We all struggle with the juggling of competing commitments and the amount of information that bombards us. Our business and work environment requires a paradoxical ability to remain centered while moving at high speed. Inevitably, things get pushed into piles, our e-mail inbox moves into triple or quadruple digits and our appointments take on the semblance of a never-ending chain of events.

I have developed a philosophy around those never-ending tasks that accumulate in my e-mail, to-do list and in piles on my desk. It is the three Ds.

- **Do** it. If it is something that can be handled right on the spot, then do it. As the adage goes, don't leave for tomorrow what you can do today. Doing it, however, means consciously leaving time in your day to handle things. It means not packing your schedule so tightly that you cannot handle those things that can easily be managed and taken care of. This frees up not only your time, but also the psychic space that having something hanging over you will consume.

- **Dump** it. Perhaps not very eloquently stated, it is nevertheless a viable strategy. How many items do you hold onto, only to find them a month later, now somehow resolved without consequence. I believe there must be a "pack rat" gene in us somewhere that has makes us hold onto so many pieces of paper "just in case", when the wisest course of action is to make a decision for the circular file. If it turns out to be the wrong decision, someone, somewhere will have a copy of it to be sure. Don't sweat it – dump it.

• **Delegate it.** Here is another tough one. It instantly triggers the "what ifs". What if someone else doesn't do it right, as well as I do, completely, etc? What if it gets lost in the shuffle? What if?

Choose to work with or hire people who are competent, dedicated and self-motivated and you will not have a problem delegating. Consider that delegating is not the same as abdicating. To delegate, make sure you are making your requests clear and specific, make sure that the person to whom you delegate work has the skills and tools to perform the work and is motivated to do their best. This is a better use of your time than doing it all yourself and at the same time, you empower others around you to take responsibility, to feel successful and to learn and grow.

Like a mantra, repeat the three D's to yourself. *Do it. Dump it. Delegate it.* When you are suddenly inspired to deal with your inbox or the piles of papers and folders on your desk, ask yourself which "D" is the right one to handle your overwhelming amount of stuff. Get used to asking yourself if you should do it now, dump it or delegate it. Like spring cleaning that happens year round, keep your outer space organized and your inner space will feel calm and harmonious as well!

"Could we change our attitude, we should not only see life differently, but life itself would come to be different."
~Katherine Mansfield

Your Four Bank Accounts

ou are a creature of habit. You have tendencies that cause you to respond the same way to similar situations and you do this without much thought to an alternative. You develop patterns so you can rely on the same solutions over and over again and mostly it works for you.

When stressed and trying to manage your time you may find that you resort to the same solution. You may decide to pay someone to clean your house so you can spend time with your family. If you have the financial means, you may buy many similar kinds of services because your time means more to you and you have the ability to pay for conveniences.

You may, on the other hand, be thrifty, preferring to spend your time instead of your money to juggle what needs to be done in your life.

It doesn't matter which you prefer. The point is that you may be defaulting to what you always do when faced with managing your life. A full and wonderful life can be better managed if you can expand your thinking about how you get things done. Different question – not "How do I do this?" but "How does this get done?"

There are four primary methods of exchange that you can use to get things done. I will call them the Four Bank Accounts. Overusing one will cause you to go bankrupt in that area. You will want to stay alert to depositing into each account to keep all of them replenished and available for you to access when you need something.

- First, there is **time**. If we had more time, we could...fill in the blank! Time seems to be the most precious commodity these days. You may decide that you enjoy cooking and want to spend your time making meals for your family, as an example.

- Second, there is **money**. A good example here is paying for housekeeping. If indeed, you do not want to withdraw from your time bank account, an option is to pay for services. This literally buys you time to spend otherwise.

- Third, is a bank account I call **resources**. You have resources and your friends have resources that if pooled and shared could help you better manage your lives. Maybe your neighbor loves to decorate and you would like to redecorate your home? Maybe the high school boy or girl next door needs a letter of recommendation in exchange for some office work. Bartering is an age-old exchange of resources that works particularly well when expectations are clearly stated.

- And last, is the account of **energy**. Using physical, mental or emotional energy can be invigorating or draining. How much energy are you willing to commit to accomplish something? And is that really where you would like to place your energy? Some examples of using your energy might be keeping in touch with friends that live far away or it could be volunteering. You reap the rewards of relationship that can be very fulfilling as you invest your energy.

Change the way you look at getting things done. Again, instead of asking, "How am I going to do this?" Ask – "How will this get done?" By asking the last question, you explore more options and can determine which bank account you can use. Don't over-withdraw from one bank account. If you do, soon enough you will be bankrupt in time, money, resources and energy. Whether it is managing your money well or managing your time, energy and resources, you can use these accounts for investing in a full and happy life that gives you what truly matters to you.

"I went back to being an amateur, in the sense of somebody who loves what she is doing. If a professional loses the love of work, routine sets in, and that's the death of work and of life."
~Ade Bethune

Beyond Layoff: Thriving

*E*veryone knows someone who has lost their job to "downsizing", "rightsizing" or whatever the euphemism of the day may be. The psychological repercussions of layoffs affect employees, their families, survivors of the layoffs and, in the end, they affect the company's long-term success.

If you have been laid off or lost your job, consider that this may not be the worst that could happen. What follows are strategies to help you cope, and eventually thrive, in the face of what you may have perceived as a devastating loss.

- **The idea of company as parent is an anachronism.** You are responsible for your career. The sooner you begin to invest in yourself, the more prepared you will be for the uncertainty of the future. You cannot control the economy or the way decisions are made in organizations. You can control your resume and your marketability. Be pro-active about your career.

- **Deal with the emotional aspects of a layoff.** You may experience a sense of betrayal. (How could this happen when I was so good at my job?). You may experience feelings of guilt (What did I do wrong?) or anger, loss, and frustration. First, understand that all these emotions are normal. Ask for assistance with handling these emotions so that they do not paralyze you or make you ill. Remember, you are not what you "do", you are not your job.

- **Look for the opportunity.** This is particularly difficult if you have not addressed the emotions that you may feel after losing your job. Yet, this may be the time for you to assess what you liked and disliked about that job and look toward choosing your future job with more purpose and a clearer idea of your value and what you need to feel successful. If possible, negotiate a severance package that gives you some financial cushion.

- **Decide what matters.** If there is one thing that most of us learned on September 11, 2001 is that every moment is precious - and tenuous. Don't grasp for what may be available "out there". Instead, look for meaningful work and intentionally "choose" the organizations with which you want to be aligned. Be the driver, not the passenger, in your career.

- **Don't do it alone.** I encourage an initial period of grieving, but then move out into the world again. Get both emotional and tangible assistance from a coach or counselor, and from friends and family. Get professional help in writing a cover letter or resume. You have about 30 seconds to get the attention of the employer. Make it count.

- **Maintain perspective.** This is not a life threatening or terminal situation. Ironically, your professional career may very well outlast the life of the company that laid you off! Although nothing is certain, you can find opportunity.

- **Set goals for yourself.** Set appropriate goals for your job search, using your values (what truly matters to you) as the standard of measurement. Work on your job search, but don't forget you have a life outside of that. Maintain your health and well being by including social, fitness and other activities that bring you happiness and benefit. You will exude health and a positive attitude and that is very attractive when it comes to interviews and networking.

• **Develop your network.** The wider you cast your "career-net", the greater your chances of success. Make a list of everyone you might consider a resource in your job search. Contact each one and convey your ideas on the type of position you would like and for which you would be qualified. Then make a direct request for assistance or a referral to someone else who might bring you closer to your next job. The Internet is a wonderful job search tool but nothing compensates for face-to-face interactions.

• **Don't get discouraged.** The average job search may last longer than you expect. Organizations don't hire according to your timetable. Their timetable is not your timetable. Don't assume the worst.

• **If you feel yourself getting frustrated, take a break.** Re-energize yourself. Re-strategize. Get another perspective from an objective person to uncover any gaps you may not be aware of.

• **Consider free agency.** Maybe you weren't cut out for the corporate 9-5 lifestyle? Collaborate with others who may be aligned with your business philosophy and with your talents and skills. Again, your personal relationships and networking skills will play an important role in your success as a free agent.

• **Never allow yourself to be disempowered by the loss of your job again.** Understand that regardless of where you go, you are always at risk of losing your job. Be sure to nurture your social as well as business contacts. Be selfish about your requirements and your personal and professional boundaries. Validate your work and your competency from the inside out. Keep a success or accomplishments log. Maintain your networking contacts and an updated resume. Doing these things will not prevent you from losing your job but having these in place will help you bounce back if you do lose your job at some point.

I've heard it said that we spend more time planning our vacations than we do planning our careers. Be pro-active about your career and be sure that your career and your job are well integrated into your life. You have a long working life ahead of you. Look for ways to bring meaning, and financial rewards, to sustain you for the journey!

"How shall I grasp it? Do not grasp it.
That which remains when there is no more grasping is the Self."
~Panchadasi

The Game

L et's talk about something I call "The Game"
and "Real Life". For the sake of this conversation let's say that the Game is the context of
what you do, what shows up externally. Real
Life is who you are authentically, your internal
make-up, at the core of who you are. Both the Game and Real
Life can contribute to your success when you have an awareness of what is truly influencing you.

The Game is culturally based with the rules and definitions governed by entities outside ourselves. It sources from
outer-directed standards from our culture or society. Real
Life is values-based, with the emphasis on hearing your soul
voice and bringing into the world all of who you truly are,
and making your choices aligned with these inner-directed
values. You then attract what you want, whether it is a relationship, clients, opportunities or alliances, according to your
inward or outer-directed focus.

An awareness of this distinction serves to help you handle challenges in a way that maintains your personal integrity (wholeness), especially when you need to make accommo-
dations or make a difficult decision. Often what you are dealing with is your interpretation of events or your judgments
about people as opposed to dealing with the event or person
itself. These interpretations are actually more a reflection of
something about you that you may not have acknowledged
than issues about someone else. You focus on what you con-
clude and what is visible to you consciously as opposed to
accepting what is actually there. If you can see your interpretations akin to looking in the mirror, you may discover something profound about yourself that leads you to a greater

sense of empowerment. You are then able to change your response to the situation from The Game perspective to acting purposefully based on what is genuine for you or the Real Life response.

This response is a thoughtful action that supports your essential values. You are not your decision, you are not your work, and you are not the person who did not get the raise or lost the contract. That is the context- The Game. This distance allows you a better perspective to make conscious choices in your life.

This distinction moves you forward, even when events seem to take you in another direction. With this awareness you begin to work on the situation, as opposed to working on your interpretation of the situation. Coming from this non-attachment you access clarity and perspective that allows for objective and values-based decisions.

A footnote: this non-attachment does not mean that you deny any emotions that you are experiencing. Emotions are a component of your humanity. There is no reason to condemn yourself for having an emotion be present. You can see and accept but not react to the emotional hook. Emotions can be expressed in healthy and safe ways without harm to yourself or others.

The distinction between "The Game" and "Real Life" opens up the ability for your life and your work to flow. You no longer struggle against the standards set outside yourself. Instead you naturally align with people, environments, and relationships that support you. Your happiness is not dependent on someone or something outside you. Your sense of worth is not based on how much money you make or where you are in a hierarchy. You gain a sense of freedom around your own destiny.

When you release these arbitrary attachments you begin to see what your true values are. And that is the beginning of designing work and life around what truly matters to you. That is the beginning of being successful according to your personal definition of success.

Next time you face a challenge, think, "I am not this situation, I just happen to be in this situation right now." BREATHE! Ask yourself if this is representative of "The Game" or "Real Life".

Choose consciously how attached you want to be. You will find more harmony, you will experience more flow and you will attract people and relationships that support your highest values when you can distinguish what is "out there" and what is "in here".

Alicia Rodriguez

"Those who say it cannot be done should not
interrupt the person doing it."
~Chinese Proverb

Conversations for Action

*T*here are conversations, then there are conversations. This is about a particular kind of conversation- one that initiates action and moves you to achieve an appropriate result. When your conversations are unfocused and haphazard, you may be having a conversation for relationship. These conversations are rapport-based and don't necessarily have any other agenda than sharing insights, information or experiences. There is nothing at all wrong with this if that is what you want. But when something is at stake, or when you need to initiate action, a conversation for rapport will not suffice.

Here are the elements for having a conversation for action that focuses you on creating a result from that interaction. This methodology works well in meetings, project management, presentations and any setting that is goal-oriented.

1. **Intention:** I can't stress this enough. You will reap exactly what you ask for so as the saying goes, "Be careful what you ask for." If your intention is to inform and educate, understand that this is a one-way conversation and that little beyond that will occur. If your conversation has been initiated for selling or marketing purposes- for instance to close a deal or get clients- then informing will not be enough. How you create the conversation to inform is very different than creating a conversation to get clients. Set the stage early by stating up front what the desired result is and how you and others will rec-

ognize the conversation as being complete. In cases of negotiation- whether it is with your spouse or with your boss- be clear about what you really want and what you are or are not willing to trade to get that outcome.

2. **Perspective:** A friend of mine, Paul Rezendes, who is a tracker in Massachusetts once told me about a concept he calls "splatter vision". It is about the kind of vision that allows him to see the signs on the ground while having an awareness of the deer standing just yards away. He speaks of the ability to basically see the details as you see the bigger picture. You need splatter vision. To have a conversation for action, you must focus on the details of your communication while communicating within the larger context of your goals and the desired action.

3. **Communication:** There are multiple ways to communicate. You communicate with your body, with your words, with your tone. Be sure that your communication is fully congruent with the action you desire. For example, to negotiate from strength you do not look at the floor and use tentative language. The appropriate use of language and metaphor can be very powerful in your conversations for action.

4. **Focus:** Your conversation for action must be structured around the result you want to achieve. Each element of the conversation must align with and support this focus. To engage in irrelevant conversation will diminish the urgency or the importance of the desired result.

5. **Completion:** Determine, on purpose, at what point the conversation is complete. Do not walk away with unspoken expectations or without asking

the other person if the conversation is complete and confirmation of the action now required. Defining the desired result and the criteria for completion at the start of the conversation will move the conversation forward and in a focused manner and will point to the conclusion when it arrives.

In work as in your life, paying attention to your intention will help you achieve the outcomes you want. You won't assume nor will the other person assume the reason for the conversation. Think of how many conversations you have had this week where you or the other person were left wondering about next steps or even if you understood one another. Understanding when to use conversations for relationship or rapport and when to use conversations for action creates understanding between you and others and empowers you to get the results you want.

"He who knows others is wise.
He who knows himself is enlightened."
~Lao Tzu

The Yin-Yang of Self

*I*n so many conversations with clients I notice a tendency toward dualism. Right or Wrong. Weak or Strong. Good or Bad. Male or Female. Heart or Mind. Assertive or Tentative.

This duality is a set-up. In looking through a lens of "either/or" you miss much of the juice in between. View yourself and your experiences in a more holistic manner. Everything and everyone plays a role. There is a time and place for each trait or response, not that one is right or the other wrong, but one is more appropriate at that given moment. Become adept at tapping into all of yourself, not just the part with which you are comfortable.

I always tell my clients that their greatest asset is their greatest liability as well. If you are very creative, you may have a tendency toward ideas but not follow through. If you are task-oriented, you may have a tendency to become mired in the details. If you are decisive and assertive, are you incorporating personal and emotional skills to communicate your objectives? You will lean on your assets so much that at some point, they become your liabilities.

You choose your style based on what you want to defend or protect or based on how comfortable you are with a particular action, belief or approach. And so, despite being proved ineffective or despite not achieving the results you seek, you still cling to your comfort zone and keep repeating the same action or you choose the same belief or approach. You choose not to venture into unfamiliar territory despite the possibility that the answer is waiting there for you. Is it better to be comfortable than successful? Are you achieving the results or finding answers doing what you have been doing?

You implement the same actions over and over and expect different results. I really love this quote by Robert Sutton, professor of Stanford Engineering School: "When you know that you need to head in a new direction, but you don't know which road to take, sometimes the best thing is to do whatever is the most ridiculous or random." At least that is one way to break the pattern. Still, you don't do this out of fear. You keep repeating the same behaviors over and over; they appear in different guises but they are the same at the core.

If you are not getting results yet feeling like you are expending much energy and effort, take a look at what you keep doing over and over. What approach do you keep repeating? What outcome do you fear will occur from doing things differently? Do you notice that this very outcome may be happening NOW while you are doing the thing you have been most comfortable doing? What is really at stake? Imagine you are at the end of the line with whatever you are doing, what could you do that would be dramatically different?

If you are at a point of total exasperation, perhaps Sutton's advice may be what you need to break through; or you may find that it will take a breakdown to achieve the breakthrough that is waiting. Consider the whole – of you, of the situation and of the results you want. Is there something missing? Get uncomfortable, do something totally different and see if you don't get more than what you are reaping now!

"There are only two ways to live your life. One is as though nothing is a miracle. The other is as though everything is a miracle."
~Albert Einstein

The Cosmic Chuckle

So what is the "cosmic chuckle" you ask? It is hard to describe, but if you are paying attention, you will notice it showing up in your life. Here is an example from a story I heard recently.

One client believes that she is not good enough for a particular job or position. She is convinced that there is more for her to do in order to be considered for a higher level position. During a social function, she meets a man and engages in conversation with him. She tells him of the work she is currently doing. He tells her how impressive her background is and asks if she would consider leaving for another position in another company. She replies that she would consider this. He takes her contact information and tells her that he will make sure that someone in this other company calls her. Within the week, she receives a call and interviews for a high-level position in this other company. She is offered the position and accepts.

On the second day at the job she meets the CEO. Guess who the CEO is? Yes, it is the man she met at the social gathering.

What is the cosmic chuckle here? First, she is open about the possibility of a higher level, more challenging position. Despite her doubt about her qualifications, she speaks openly and confidently about the work she has been doing. She is being authentic when she meets the man and thus makes an impression on him. She doesn't even know his position. The Universe seems to conspire in challenging her belief that she is not yet good enough by presenting this opportunity in disguise.

In Native American tradition there is Kokopelli, the trickster that is in charge of what I call the cosmic chuckle. You may have seen an image of this figure playing a flute. He is the one that through magic and trickery reveals the shadow side in a humorous way.

Sometimes, when you are bound by your beliefs or your doubts or are in the process of shifting these, something occurs in your experience that validates this new way of being. It may appear as a chance meeting or perhaps a new way of listening to a song or something you read or a possibility that challenges your belief of self.

When you are paying attention, you begin to see that there are these cosmic chuckles that have you laugh at yourself as you begin to notice that indeed, something has shifted into a new way of being and behaving. In recognizing this, you can then fully step into this new chapter, fully owning all of who you are becoming. Your powerful self is emerging!

Start noticing what needs to shift for you. What is it that you believe about yourself that limits you? What in your life challenges this belief? Are you ready to fully step up into a new empowered self? That is when the cosmic chuckle may appear in your life, validating the evolving you while chuckling away at your doubts.

"In the esoteric Judaism of the Cabalah, the Deep Self
is named the Neshamah, from the root of Shmhm,
'to hear or listen': the Neshamah is She Who Listens,
the soul who inspires or guides us."
~Starhawk

Inspiration

*T*here are times when I notice a word repeatedly shows up in my life or work. This word,
recently, is *inspiration*. As a coach I notice
words and distinctions in language that can at first appear
subtle, but are indeed quite powerful. So I began to consider
the words inspiration and motivation. One dictionary defines
inspire as "to arouse in someone". The definition for motivate
is "to give incentive".

I see inspiration as something that truly does arise from
within, perhaps as a catalyst from the outside, but inspiration
sources from within. Motivation appears to be driven by
external forces, like incentives, or even fear sometimes.

Consider how much more powerful it is to inspire
someone as opposed to motivate someone. Inspiration
does not require an outside force; it flows without struggle
and it draws us toward something. This is more powerful
than motivation, whose progress may depend on the
outside stimulation or incentive. Once that is removed,
are you still motivated?

When you are inspired it is effortless and you flow
toward a positive result. Many times motivation sources
from the fear of something or the lack of something. It
pushes you toward a goal that tends to be temporal in nature
and once achieved, no longer holds any value.

Inspiration suggests a creative element and imagination.
Inspiration can also suggest a spiritual element, something
that is born from your soul voice calling to you to manifest an

idea, dream or vision. Inspiration evokes emotions, energizes you and provokes action. When you are creating, inspiration moves you through the difficult and uncomfortable place of uncertainty and not knowing. It sustains you through doubts and obstacles.

Consider how your style, presence or language affects those around you. Are you inspiring them or motivating them? Which would you prefer to do? How might it be different if you moved into a place where you were able to inspire in others greater potential than they may have believed of themselves? How would this affect the level of commitment to a vision or goal? What would change about the intensity and passion for a person's life or work?

What shifts would need to occur for you so that you could inspire others? What role does inspiration play in your life. How do you inspire others? Language, music, productions, teaching, what else? Look around you for others that may inspire you.

Remember, each time you touch someone in your day is an opportunity to inspire and be inspired if you are open to the extraordinary in the ordinary. Pay attention. Stay in touch with your inner world. Be generous and inspiration will find you.

"F" is for Focus

Y ou live in a time when the speed of business and life is so fast, and the amount of information coming at you is so great, that maintaining focus and paying attention is more than difficult. One of the reasons you do not accomplish the goals you set for yourself is due to this inability to focus amidst all the chaos and noise.

It is not about ability but instead it is about paying attention to paying attention. Does that make sense? Read it again. It is about paying attention to paying attention. You have the ability; you may, however, become distracted to the point of confusion and paralysis.

Here are some ways to maintain focus.

• Many successful CEO's I know only schedule about 40 percent of their time. The rest of their time is available to deal with issues that arise and to reflect and strategize. Successful leaders operate in the quadrant of important/not urgent. This allows them to have long-range vision on issues that are important but not necessarily urgent. Crisis management exists in the quadrant of important/urgent. Too much time here causes burn out and creates the environment for faulty decision-making.

• How much time are you spending in the important/urgent quadrant? How can you move into the important/not urgent quadrant? Answer: don't over-schedule yourself. Keep time in your day to work strategically on achieving your goals and time for quiet reflection. This allows you to move forward bit by bit and still work tactically during the day. You retain focus because the time you set aside is a consistent and regular behavior specifically for thinking and reflection. You will notice that actions derived from this time are more targeted and successful.

• Remember, just as you can only be in one place at one time, you can only focus on one thing at one time. Be there in the moment with what is present, dealing with it, and then move to the next moment. Trying to be in multiple mental or psychic places at the same time doesn't work. Deal with each link in the time chain moving from one link to another smoothly when you are complete. This presence supports focus. One moment, then another moment, then another moment leads you to the inevitable conclusion. By focusing on what action is needed from moment to moment you will reach your goal without feeling drained and fatigued.

• There is a difference between something that draws you forward and something that pushes you away. For example, if you are in a career transition, are you approaching this as a way to leave your current job (pushing away) or as a way to create a life and work around what matters most to you (drawing you forward)? There is a very different energy contained in each of these approaches. You will flow toward the creation of new work but you will get stuck on the road of running away from the current situation. Think in terms of moving toward something as opposed to moving away from something and you will be better able to maintain focus.

• Creative people, in particular, have difficulty maintaining focus. When I ask my most creative clients what gets in the way, they inevitably point to all the ideas that they conceive and the distractions that this generates. An effective solution is to create an idea folder where the ideas can be captured for a later date. Knowing that these ideas are available for implementation later is likely to appease the creative mind and provides fodder for new projects.

• Focus does not mean the exclusion of other tasks, ideas or projects. Focus means that <u>for now</u> you will *concentrate* your efforts on one task, idea or project. Think of a magnifying glass. When the rays of the sun pass through the magnifying glass, they narrow and ignite the paper on the other side. That does not mean that the sunlight around the magnifying glass is extinguished. Such is the same with focus. You still have other things to do, but your energy, time and resources are concentrated on one thing.

• Create an orientation first, and then use a powerful question to help you to decide minute by minute how you will use your time, energy and resources. For example, I want to increase sales by $5000 this month. That becomes the orientation. The focusing question that one would ask when confronted with options on how to spend one's time might be: what action or behavior brings me closer to my goal of +$5K? You orient your actions around your desired result. You will make better decisions with greater ease and maintain focus.

• If your goal is to have a committed relationship, this also works. What actions, beliefs or approaches will bring you closer to meeting someone who is interested in a committed relationship with you? Your choice becomes much clearer and your chances of accomplishing this increase.

• Having choice is a wonderful thing, but in today's culture you are barraged with too many choices, making it difficult to choose. Sounds like a cosmic chuckle to me! If you find yourself paralyzed by the choices, funnel them down to two choices. You may have options but ultimately the brain can only choose from two options. If you have four possibilities (A, B, C, and D) first choose between A and B (B). Then choose between C and D (C). Now choose between B and C. Bring your many choices down to only two and eliminate your analysis/paralysis.

• Which came first, the chicken or the egg? This is what I would call a Western koan. The answer is: Yes! Ultimately, you end up making it all up anyway, so decide and take action, moving in the direction of your goals and dreams.

• Another powerful question that I keep posted in writing near my workstation helps me to return to what really matters most to me. What I wrote is: "How do I really want to be spending this one moment?" It allows me to be very conscious of the choices I make with my time and efforts and it reminds me that I am at choice. I may choose to do something I don't really want to do, but I am choosing on purpose and mindfully. That is a much more powerful way to choose than to be reactionary or scattered.

You may have big plans, but without intention, focus, structure, support and action, they may well remain just that – plans. It starts with the quality of attention. The higher the quality of attention, the more focus, the more assured you are of designing your work and life around what truly matters to you.

"Keep your thoughts positive, because your thoughts become your words. Keep your words positive, because your words become your behavior. Keep your behavior positive, because your behavior becomes your habits. Keep your habits positive, because your habits become your values. Keep your values positive, because your values become your destiny."
~Mahatma Gandhi

Positive Action: Personal Destiny

*T*oo often we can all slip into negativity and what I call the "ain't it awfuls". When you are tired, when you are overwhelmed, it is so easy to lose sight of the abundance that is present right in front of you. There is a Persian saying: "I cried because I had no shoes until I met a man who had no feet." Sometimes it takes a moment to look outside of your situation long enough to realize what is truly there for you. Sometimes it takes being with another person who "has no feet" for you to realize that you are truly blessed.

A good life is not necessarily a life absent of conflict and pain. It is in conflict and pain that you may experience your greatest moments. These are moments of true courage, deep faith, unconditional love and personal evolution. But it is only with self-awareness and time for reflection that you can maintain that calm center even in the midst of the greatest storm.

Your business may be off, you may be experiencing hardship, someone you know may be ill. These are realities. But expand that reality and make room for what is possible. If your business is slow, what does this open time allow you to do that you have not been able to do or what issues can be addressed in this quiet time? If you are experiencing hardship, how might you simplify your life in ways that require less consumption of time, money or energy? If someone you know is ill, can you give them the gift of presence, laughter or witnessing that they might forget their illness for a while and return to their essential self? If you are feeling overwhelmed, how might you bring joy and quiet into this busy space?

Being of service to another is a nurturing action. It nurtures someone else and nurtures you. Even more importantly in times of stress nurturing yourself can support your journey.

Reflect now for a moment on what thoughts, words, behaviors, habits and values you will manifest that will determine your personal destiny. It is your journey – how will you determine its quality?

"Sometimes your joy is the source of your smile, but sometimes your smile can be the source of your joy."
~Thich Nhat Hanh

What Makes You Smile

*P*eople come to coaching for many, many reasons. Some are working through a transition in their lives, moving from a place called here to an unknown place they call there. Others want to change, enhance, get more of, or get less of something. Still other people are looking to evolve themselves, either spiritually, personally or professionally.

More and more leaders are turning to coaching to become more effective, to inspire their organization and its people, and to live to their own full potential. Recently a coach/friend of mine answered the question "What is coaching about?" His response was "Being fully human". As a coach, I agree with this.

What does it mean to be fully human? It may mean different things to different people at different stages in their lives. As you go through your life (read: age, mature, evolve, develop, etc.) what truly matters to you changes. What may have been terribly important in your twenties is an echo compared to what may be important in your forties.

How do you become aware of these subtle shifts? What occurs when one day you awaken to a dissatisfaction with how you are living? How do you rediscover your passion for life, for work, for people? How do you reconnect with your essential self? How will you know what direction to travel?

It is about remembering those moments in your life that have made you smile. To remember in every cell of your body is to touch a past experience that has brought you joy. Don't underestimate joy. It is a powerful experience that you remember on a cellular level. It is a clue to what makes you happy.

When looking to reconnect with that joyful and playful person inside, simply pay attention to what makes you smile as you journey through your day. It means slowing down a bit in order to savor the moments in a way that allows you to sense joy, happiness or humor. And when you feel this, you will automatically smile. That is your clue to what may inspire you. That is your clue to what you could be doing now to be happier and to create more meaning in your life. The answer to joy is right there – you only have to smile!

A Wisdom Practice: P B C R

*R*ecently I heard a report on the news: Stress contributes to the aging process. All I could think of was what my son says when he hears something that is so obvious: "Duh!" And although I really hate that term, that is exactly what popped into my mind. I kept thinking, who paid for this report? Of course we all know stress contributes to aging!

I would like to share with you a practice I give to my clients that I also practice in times of stress. This could be when conflict arises, when something unpredictable occurs or even when I am tired and my son is not behaving as I believe he should (but I don't want to "lose it" on him!).

This practice is applicable to many situations. Situations where it works best are: stressful situations, situations that require clear thinking, situations that deal with conflict, or when you are moving quickly from one task to another. It is *"Pause, Breathe, Center, Respond"*. It takes about three seconds – the amount of time it takes to pause, take a very deep breath in, hold for a second, exhale completely, and come back to one's inner center before responding to the person or to the event. Physiologically, it relaxes the body and the oxygen intake clears the brain. It also creates enough space (in the pause) to be able to respond thoughtfully rather than to enter into a habitual reaction. An example: "Mary" was presenting to her directors on a new marketing plan. After presenting, one senior manager attacked the plan and attempted to provoke her into a reactionary response. She did not respond immediately even though she felt personally attacked. She quietly paused, breathed and centered herself, and was able to respond with great clarity and confidence, without any acrimony or defensiveness. Her plan was approved. Another example: "Mike" moves quickly in his day from meeting to meeting to the point that he was losing track of what he wanted to actually accomplish in each meeting. By the end of the day he was exhausted and feeling as if he had not accomplished anything. By practicing the four-part PBCR between meetings, he was able to complete his thinking on one meeting, pause, and shift to focus on the desired outcome of the following meeting. He was more productive, more engaged in each meeting, he made better decisions, communicated more effectively and he felt energized, not drained, by the pace of his day.

As you go through your day, practice P-B-C-R. It will allow you to remain focused, it will keep you from habitual responses that do not have positive results and it will maintain your body as well as your mind.

Now: Pause – Breathe – Center - Respond

Chapter Five
Beginnings and Endings

"Orientation:
A change in position in response to external stimulus"
~Merriam Webster Dictionary

Soul-Centered Compass

*Y*ou can find yourself feeling very busy, but not necessarily productive. You may also discover that you are on auto pilot, just wanting to get through the day, without really thinking about whether or not you are actually doing what you need to do or want to do in your life. Perhaps you may even discover that you have put your dreams on hold for the sake of a definition of success that you have not evaluated recently.

Throughout your personal evolution and as you age and move through life transitions, your values change. What I mean by values is: what really matters to you. Yet, you continue on the same path as before, a path based on outdated beliefs, on your past reality and motivated by goals created by others, or even yourself, that are no longer relevant. At what point, then, do you stop and re-assess your life?

You may notice a weariness or tiredness that I describe as being tired from the inside out. You may begin to lose optimism. You may become angry and combative or distant in your relationships. And finally, you may lose faith and hope. These are indications to STOP!

If you do not stop voluntarily, something will happen to make you stop. I have seen this time and time again. These events are powerful, even devastating. They cause you to see yourself essentially, devoid of all the trappings of how you define yourself in the outside world. You get a glimpse of your mortality. You see your impermanence. You begin to see that you are a single drop in a very large ocean.

It is from this awareness that you have the opportunity to re-orient your life around what really does matter to you

NOW. Like a ship that has gone off course, you can use your internal soul compass to put yourself back on the true course of your life.

Your true north is the center point of your life at this time. It provides an internal origin point from which you generate the actions that affect other areas of your life. It creates a congruency and flow between the aspects of your life that are important to you now.

You move from that centered, internal point, this genuine way of being, and you carry this into everything in your life. It permeates your thoughts, behaviors and actions. It has a particular flow.

Think of the planetary system. Planets gravitate around the Sun. Planets move in alignment with the Sun and they are interacting with the forces of the Sun. They are influenced by the Sun as the center-point. This is analogous to Orientation.

Imagine that the Sun is your center-point; it is where you get your bearings. Imagine that the planets are what you value. One planet may be work, another may be community, another can be financial wellbeing, another family and so on and so on. All of these planets orient around your sun, or what truly matters to you. How does what matters to you manifest in each one of these planets? How do you live your values through your community, family, finances and whatever you choose to circle this sun?

The Center Circle holds the common element that must be present in all aspects of one's life in order to have all the circles align and flow. It is the "source" behind your decisions, your actions and your beliefs. It speaks to HOW you would like to BE in the other aspects of your life. It is not a Doing. The center is a way of Being.

Here is an example. One client told me he had three main areas in his life: his Business, his Family and his Industry. The values he associated with these were (Business) Financial Security, (Family) Legacy and (Industry) Service. There was

---

one common element that was the source of how he interacted with Business, Family and Industry. For him, that word or orientation was Freedom. It was critical that he be "free" in his life. He oriented around being Free. So if a business decision tied him in ways that he was not free to be with his Family, or affect his Finances or contribute to his Industry, then he would make an alternative choice or negotiate the conditions. He aligned each aspect of his life around being free.

Another client, a woman, decided to move from an orientation around Career and Work (sense of accomplishment) to an orientation around her Family (she described it as "being present"). Having this new orientation affected decisions made in the family's finances, time they spent on hobbies or travel and other areas in their lives.

The number and names of areas or values (circles or planets as I have described them) does not matter as long as they are meaningful to you and you feel a commitment to these. When you align with what is true for you, with how you know you want to *be* in the world, life moves from struggle to flow. You are calmer, you are more focused and you experience more meaning in your life and work. Even if there is difficulty, it does not feel the same as struggle.

Notice how you are or are not in alignment with your sun or orientation. Ask yourself what you can do to create more alignment, more flow from that source in your life. How can you take that sense of being into every aspect of your life? Please know that this may take days or weeks for you to complete. Be gentle with yourself and honor your Truth. Then steer your life back on course to create life and work that brings you joy and fulfillment.

"I think what we're seeking is an experience of being alive,
so that our life experiences on the purely physical plane
will have resonance within our own innermost being
and reality, so that we actually feel
the rapture of being alive."
~Joseph Campbell

Transitions:
Re-Inventing Yourself

You are constantly evolving as you experience your world. The question becomes, are you *aware* of changes in attitudes, needs, beliefs and desires? What you may want at the age of 20 may be very different than what you want at 30, 40 or 60.

You may have already outgrown yourself before recognizing that you are anchored in your past. You begin to feel uncomfortable, anxious, sometimes disillusioned. Your friends or family may tell you that you should be happy with what you have, that you shouldn't "rock the boat". So you deny that funny feeling in your gut and keep working at whatever it is that you should be working at. You grow more and more unhappy until you can't even stand to be with yourself, let alone with anyone else.

If you are lucky, something will intervene to demonstrate that there really is something that needs to shift for you to be happy. You become aware that it is time to re-invent yourself on purpose. You are already in the blueprint stage even if you are not consciously aware of it.

Are you feeling an unexplainable sadness in your day? Is getting up in the morning a struggle? Are you dissatisfied with your job, career or relationships? These may be signs that a shift is under way. What can you do to move from this place of malaise to a place where you can live more purposefully?

• **Find time to be still.** I mean still, not quietly reading a newspaper but still in your mind and actions. Meditation is a great means to calm your mind. If you find you can't sit still that long, you may be someone who finds stillness in action. Go for a run, go kayaking, take a walk and in this physical activity your mind may move out of the way for you to be still internally. Nature is a wonderful partner in stillness: find some water, a lake, river or ocean, and listen to the sound of the water against the shore. Listen with your heart. What is it telling you?

• **Pay attention.** As you go through your day, notice how you feel. Do you feel something is missing? Look not only for the emptiness, but pay attention to those people, events, places or things that make you smile or relax. These are clues to what makes you happy.

• **Give yourself permission.** Permission to let go of those patterns which no longer serve you, permission to do things completely radical (for you), permission to be with whatever or whoever makes you happy.

• **Elevate your standards**. When you have measured your happiness by one standard, it becomes difficult to create a new standard if you are still holding on to the old one. Don't feel guilt about getting what you want just because it wasn't what you wanted before or what you thought you should want.

• **Eliminate what drains you of energy.** Scrutinize where your energy is going. If you are tolerating something in your life that no longer serves you, it is time to put it away. Like cleaning out your closets; you throw away clothes you haven't worn for years or are out of style to make room for the new stuff.

• **Old patterns are hard to break.** The old patterns will try to re-assert themselves when you meet an obstacle. It will be the familiar place to go, but not the right place any longer. Don't beat yourself up if you falter. Renew your commitment, get back in touch through stillness and move on.

• **Enjoy the new you.** What you may find is that there is no "new" you, but the memory of who you are essentially has now returned. You will be more comfortable and happy if you are living by your own values and standards, than if you are living by someone else's. The world will open up to you differently than before. You will feel more alive and engaged.

This being human is an evolutionary process. Don't be afraid to step into your own evolution. Listen to your inner pilot to guide you through transitions and you will find the life you were meant to lead at this moment. Feel the rapture of being alive!

"There is only one courage and that is the courage to go on dying to the past, not to collect it, not to accumulate it, not to cling to it. We all cling to the past, and because we cling to the past we become unavailable to the present."
~Bhagwan Shree Rajneesh,
"Walking in Zen, Sitting in Zen"

Habitual Responses

*P*ay attention!

You really don't. You go through your day or week in crisis management mode, putting out one fire after another. You are poorly equipped to handle long-range planning or even appropriate prioritizing when you are distracted by what perceived emergencies.

Under stressful conditions, or under conditions where you are not focused, you are apt to fall into *habitual patterns*. These patterns are developed over time and become so subtle that you no longer see them as *habitual responses*. Your awareness of doing any one thing by rote is only apparent when someone points this out to you. These habitual responses are the result of being tired, overwhelmed, unfocused, afraid or threatened. You unconsciously choose the path of least resistance, even if this is not the most beneficial or productive choice.

It is difficult to stay present to your current environment while chaos is all around. You get caught up and react instead of respond. In doing so, you remain in dysfunctional relationships, you miss potential business opportunities and you maintain the cycle of stress.

How can you choose or decide more consciously so that you can maintain your emotional, physical and mental equilibrium?

Here are ten suggestions for you to think about:

- **Learn to identify true emergencies from false urgencies.** One habitual response is to accept from others, without your own assessment, that something is an emergency just because someone else says it is so. A client calls with what they feel is an immediate concern. Ask questions first, review your availability and determine if this is really urgent or if there is another alternative response time. Ask first, and then respond thoughtfully.

- **Allow space and time for true emergencies.** You may be over-committed, which makes it even more difficult to deal with the real emergencies. Be sure to allow more than enough resources in terms of support, energy and time to be able to handle the unexpected without compromising your well-being or your priorities.

- **Learn ways of remaining centered in the midst of great activity.** Find ways to center or calm yourself even in the midst of chaos. One thing that is true today is that everything is constantly changing. The paradox is how to stay still and centered while in motion. I envision being the eye of the tornado. Keep a physical reminder on your desk or within your range of vision (an inspirational message, a picture, a candle, a water fountain, a stone you can hold in your hand are some suggestions) that supports your holding your center in the midst of chaos.

- **Re-frame how you prioritize or make choices.** You may feel that saying "no" to someone is hurtful or not supportive. If you have trouble using this powerful two-letter word, reframe the response. Try asking more questions to determine what is really

---

Alicia Rodriguez

needed. Try delegating to someone else or referring to someone else. And try to create space in which to think about your response by saying, "Let me get back to you on this", or "Let me think about this" or "Let me double check my availability." This says "yes" to you and teaches you to break out of the habitual pattern of saying "yes" to everyone and everything.

• **Be aware of your body. Your body is wise.** When you are too busy to listen, or under duress, your body will send you signals. Your breathing will change, your posture will shift and if you ignore the signals, you will get ill. By tuning into your body, especially your breathing, you can remain relaxed, focused and better able to make decisions.

• **Don't sweat the small stuff.** You could be getting bogged down in mundane details that consume and drain you. Assess and eliminate what drains you. Orient around your priorities and you will be less apt to wander into habitual responses. Setting priorities and releasing "the small stuff" will reduce habitual responses.

• **The past does not dictate the future.** When confronted today with a situation like one yesterday, you may gravitate to what has worked in the past without thought to the new conditions. This, too, is a habitual response. By evaluating the situation based on current realities, you move out of habitual assumptions and responses. Fresh perspectives, innovations and opportunities become apparent.

• **Get an outside perspective.** Sometimes what you think you know is worse than not knowing at all. You may be limited by what you think you know.

Getting an outside, objective person to point out your behaviors or to reflect back to you your thought process, may be enough to rouse you into more thoughtful patterns.

• **Release your fear of failure.** Habitual responses are in themselves a response to your fear of failure. It feels safer to react in the same manner than to change your reaction. In changing your reactions you break the dynamic that exists. Your fear may be the loss of a relationship, hurting someone's feelings, and heaven forbid, just plain making the wrong decision. Failure is only failure if you don't learn from it and move on. Failure is indeed, information that you need to make adjustments.

• **An easy way to avoid the unpleasant.** If you look closely at some of your habitual patterns or responses you will find that you are avoiding something. As an example, saying "I am tired." may be your response to avoiding conflict or a difficult conversation. Another example: One client responded to critiques of her work by diminishing someone else's work. She was unaware of doing this, wondering why her work relationships were tenuous, until we replayed these types of situations word per word. She has since adapted language to help her respond thoughtfully and not react defensively.

It takes courage and support to break out of habitual responses and patterns. There is always the fear that something more is at stake. What you stand to lose is really old, limiting ways of being and stress. Focus on what you stand to gain by breaking the habitual cycles you have created. Innovative solutions, well being, values-oriented decisions and life-on-purpose are the real elements you stand to gain!

"We are what we think. All that we are arises with our thoughts.
With our thoughts we make our world."
~Buddha

Old Patterns for
New Ways of Being

*R*egardless of how you try to change, old patterns will try to re-assert themselves when you meet an obstacle. It will be the familiar place to go, but not the right place any longer.

Old patterns are based in very subtle and deeply- rooted belief systems. These are so integrated that you may be unable to recognize them in yourself. When you become uncomfortable, or threatened, you fall back on patterns of behavior which may have served you in the past, but which no longer serve you. When you re-design your life you need to create new patterns which serve your new priorities and which support living at a more evolved level.

For example, you may shift from a dependency on caffeine and adrenaline into a perspective of health and well-being using exercise, nutrition and sleep to energize you. But in a deadline crunch you may forego those self-care values and revert to patterns using caffeine or adrenaline to meet your work demands.

In business, you may evolve into being vision-directed and consciously choosing your clients, vendors and associates from a perspective of alignment with your values. Again, in times of economic slowdown, you may feel compelled to take any contract or job for the income. It is easy to stay the course when there is abundance; it is more difficult when you feel scarcity.

You compromise the long-range vision and may eventually lose money, accepting work that is not appropriate to your goals. In both cases, you choose out of fear and this causes conflict, and in the long run, creates a cycle of stress, exhaustion and perhaps financial hardship. *You cannot sustain positive results with negative behaviors.*

The solution to your dependency on old patterns is this:

1. **Be aware** that when you hit obstacles, you will gravitate to what is familiar, even if it is not the right thing to do. Pay attention.

2. **Anticipate potential obstacles** with the help of a coach, friend or partner. Create solutions based on your new vision or goal as the focus for your choice. Plan positive solutions in advance of potential obstacles so you are prepared when they arrive.

3. **Develop support systems** around you that nudge you into keeping up healthy, productive patterns. Exercise with a friend, post your vision and mission statement, network with individuals operating on a higher level.

4. **Consistently review your personal and professional vision** to confirm that your choices are aligned with it. This periodic review will keep you focused and will inform you when it does become time to adjust your course or make another shift or transition.

5. **Don't beat yourself up** if you fall back into old patterns. Recognize that you may be transitioning from one chapter into the next and that this is all part of the process.

Your life is dynamic and if you are living with attention and intention, you will embrace transitions and shifts with excitement and passion.

Alicia Rodriguez

"Courage is not the towering oak that sees storms come and go;
it is the fragile blossom that opens in the snow."
~Alice M. Swaim in
"The Change-Your-Life" Quote Book by Allen Klein

What If?

With the arrival of each new year come the inevitable "resolutions". But resolutions don't work. Two reasons why they don't work are 1) They don't really address the true source of a problem, they address a symptom, and 2) Resolutions are more driven by what you do not want in your life than by what you do want in your life.

You start by trying to solve something using your mind. But to get to what really matters, to reach for your dreams, you need to instead look through the eyes of the soul. These eyes see a different picture. These eyes are seeking that which brings meaning into our lives.

The soul sees beyond the things you have been told you should have or should do. This approach requires inaction versus action. To really see and hear, you need to pay attention. In order to pay attention, you need to slow down. You need to be still long enough to become fully alive.

When you can finally hear your soul voice and see through the eyes of your soul, you may become frightened and anxious at first. "How could I possibly want that?" "What if I try and I fail?" "What if they think ill of me or think that I am being selfish." or "What if I look stupid?" Ah, there is the mind and ego, interfering again! The mind and ego are very well intentioned. After all, these partners created very successful strategies to protect you along the way.

With your mind, and with your ego, you develop all sorts of patterns, habits and compensating strategies that help adapt and succeed with minimum pain. You are safe. You know your limitations and excel within those, not venturing too far into unknown territory. You become adept in your version of reality. And then one day, you wake up. You see a life, a safe life, but one without passion. You hunger for evolution but are afraid to step out into the unknown. "What if?"

When you hear yourself utter these words, "What If?" either out loud or silently, know that fear has arrived. Your mind will try to protect you; it will rationalize why you should not step out of your comfort zone. It will demand that the same pattern of your life continue, because you are kept safe that way. But the method used is fear.

Fear will keep you from stepping out because "What if...they don't like me anymore? What if...I fail? What if...I look stupid? What if I actually get what I have always wanted?" Oh, gosh, not that! That flies in the face of everything you have ever been taught!

"What if...?" keeps you from taking even the first step toward your dream. It takes you out of the present and into a future dictated by fear as if it were the inevitable outcome. You fill the "what if...?" with requirements that really don't matter. All that is required is that you take the first step putting one foot in front of the other. In the present there is no requirement to succeed, to look good, or to be the best. The only requirement of your dream is to be here and take the step.

Next time you hear, "What if...?" when you venture out of your comfort zone to reach for your dream, don't back down. Name the fear. Write down each and every "What if...?" that you hear. Be honest, don't edit. And at the end of your list, go back and read each and every one OUT LOUD. Your soul will answer simply.

Nothing your mind can imagine could possibly be as frightening as living a life half-lived or flat-lining through your life. Your soul knows this. Taking on the "What if's" takes courage, but the price of not blossoming into your full life is to whither in the snow.

This Old House

*T*he house we owned in Boston was old. Two years after we bought it, we surrendered to the reality that the house needed to be completely rewired. Not that we had oodles of electronics, but we had enough to tax the electrical system of the old Colonial. We spent literally years living with numerous outages, and we were wearing a path to the circuit breakers. Finally, we concluded that indeed all the demands of the numerous electrical devices we had in the house were too much for a system designed in the 1960s when most families owned perhaps a TV or two, but no computers, dishwashers, Play Stations, or large refrigerators. It was time to re-wire the house!

And it was not fun. Our house took about a week to re-wire. When the electrician came to do the work, he found wires in places we had not anticipated, some were dangerously bare and much did not meet code. That transitional period, between the way it was and the new system was uncomfortable and inconvenient.

Now you must be wondering, why the heck is she talking about electrical wiring? It occurred to me that this was a good metaphor for personal development. You are much like an old house. You are built as well as can be expected at the time. Gradually, as you age or as you enter into different life phases, new demands are placed on you. And you begin to experience breakdowns – breakdowns in your relationships, in your performance at work, or in your health and well being.

You are operating under more duress, with the same resources (electrical system) you had before. You are not prepared to meet these new demands and in trying to meet this additional stress using old methodologies, beliefs or patterns, you encounter breakdowns, confusion and discomfort.

One day you decide – "time to rewire the house". This just isn't working. It's time to install new systems to meet the new demands. Perhaps, it may even be time to re-invent yourself in ways that have you function more optimally in your new environment or life phase.

This can be a painful process. For a while you function even worse than before. For a while things are disconnected and confusing. And even as the new system is installed, there may be occasional "kinks" to work out.

But there comes a day when you know that it was worth it. When you now have this new installed system (as a friend says – a shift in your WOB – way of being) and you can better meet the demands of your life and work. The connections are finally made, linking one thing to another in a way that is efficient and makes sense. You can think more clearly, function more effectively and feel more accomplished experiencing a greater sense of inner peace.

The house is still the same old house. The difference is in the installation of new systems. You do not have to tear down the house. You only have to become aware of the new demands and the opportunity to grow into something better than before. Trusting the process, believing in the new possibility and keeping your eye on the outcome will help ease you through the transition.

So, is it time to rewire your Old House?

"If you ask me what I have come to do in this world,
I will reply: 'I am here to live aloud.'"
~ Emile Zola

Renewing Who I Am

*I*n one coaching session a client of mine was discussing what was next for her and what goals she wanted to set. She was unable to visualize or even name what that was. Typically, if you can name a goal, you can visualize and achieve it. We ended up with a conversation about labels placed on people, jobs and careers. Not only do you label these but you attach assumptions about what it means to be a doctor, teacher, mother, wife, CEO, (or whatever) to these – assumptions that create beliefs that you live as truths. And based on these beliefs you decide whether or not that is someone you could be, without considering that this assumption may be based on how someone else is living that role. What you miss is that this doesn't mean that you must live that role in that same way. This way of thinking excludes the who you are and focuses only on what you believe that label is, how that type of life is lived and what you can bring to that role. And in doing this, you remove the focus of Who I Am and we move into Who I Am Not. As an example, (stereotypically) a teacher is someone who is compassionate, routine-oriented, likes kids, enjoys having the summers off, and whatever else you may conceive. A doctor is someone who is ambitious, who is clinical in his/her approach to the world, who deals only with empirical information and whatever else you may conceive. A CEO is tough, cannot show emotion, values competition and again you make assumptions. Your stereotypes of roles keep you from the possibility of redefining who you are or could be in those roles.

I know many teachers who may encompass many of the named traits but who have indeed traveled the world, are very experiential and not book-oriented, who believe that the best teachers are kinesthetic and more. And I know many doctors who believe in healing through prayer as an adjunct to medicine, who volunteer time and energy to community and who are some of the most compassionate people I know. I know CEO's who are highly relational and collaborative.

So what is the difference? The difference is that the role you take, the job you find, the career you choose is DEFINED BY WHO YOU ARE; *it is not the other way around. You are not defined by what you do or your role or job.* The mistake you make when you are choosing your career is that you do not acknowledge that first you must know who you are and from there, from the magic and gifts, talents and interests you embody, you choose your work.

If you say "I AM THIS", are you also saying "I AM NOT THAT"? If you say you are a teacher, do you believe you are also saying that you cannot be spontaneous, cannot bring all of who you are to your work? If you say you are a CEO, do you believe you are also saying that you cannot be collaborative, that you cannot show empathy and emotion, that you cannot lead others by nurturing them? Can a scientist then not be poetic? In defining who I am, am I also defining who I am not based on my assumptions?

Here was my big "AHA!" You may define who you are by first defining who you are not based on the labels and assumptions that you have been taught over the course of your life. "I am not this or that, therefore I could never be a teacher, a doctor, a lawyer, a baseball player, a parent." And that way is a killer of dreams. That is the child who played at being an astronaut but was told he/she could never be that because being an astronaut is unrealistic. That is the young girl who loved to draw and paint or write but was told that artists make no money, are not appreciated and why don't you pick a career where you can earn a good living. Sound familiar?

What labels do you put on yourself and others? What are

the assumptions behind those labels? Where did the labels and assumptions come from? What do you believe that wearing that label says about who you are or who you are not? Are you looking at your life and work from an inclusive lens of possibilities that sees all of who you are genuinely; or are you only peering through a tube that sees only the label and what that means, exclusive of what lies outside of that tunnel, exclusive of your magic, your gifts, your passions and all that you may bring to that role?

My gift to you is a question. Be thoughtful about your answer. But before moving on be sure to get clear on the answer.

"What keeps you from your greatness?"

Whispers of New Beginnings

I have to admit to getting bored every two or three years. I love what I do, please understand. However, I thrive on a challenge and when it seems like things are going smoothly, I upset the cart somewhat on purpose, just to see what shakes out. I am ever surprised at the outcomes!

I am one person who really does notice when I begin to feel stagnant. I notice it in my body first. I fatigue easily, I start getting up late – even late for me – and I begin to make poor choices. By poor choices I mean choices that are not aligned with anything in particular. So my energy tends to get scattered and I lose my sense of accomplishment. That is another indicator for me.

Once I recognize that I am in a space where something internally is coming to an end, I also begin to actively seek out a new possibility even though I don't know what it is. I begin to listen differently and pay attention more. I notice synchronicity and because I am in a state of openness and possibility a casual conversation may then become a possibility for learning or for a shift in direction or a new goal. And historically, there has always been something waiting there to be discovered.

Is it time for you to open up to something new, even if you don't know what it is? How are you feeling in your work and life? I am not talking about a "mid-life crisis" scenario; I am talking about an evolutionary phase in your spiritual development or your personal life or your business or work. Pay attention to even the ordinary things. Sometimes greatness does not yell, it whispers. And only by recognizing the end of one thing, the beginning of something else and the openness in between, will you actually hear the whisper.

Chapter Six
Seasons

"One has just to be oneself. That's my basic message.
The moment you accept yourself, as you are,
all burdens, all mountainous burdens, disappear.
Then life is a sheer joy, a festival of lights."
~Bhagwan Shree Rajneesh,
The Sound of One Hand Clapping

Souls Blooming in Springtime

*T*ake a moment to smell the air. Ah, spring is coming. In some places, like here in Annapolis, the daffodils and tulips are out. Bunnies have come out of the brush just in time for Easter. Catholics celebrate Easter as the time when Jesus rose from the dead. Mother Nature nudges her flowers out of the earth as well. Everywhere around us the sleepy are rising. Are you? Are you sleeping? Or are you awake now? Do your days seem the same, moving from one day to the next and, from one month to the next, without any passion or energy? Or do you really wake up every morning and yell to the world, "I am alive, I have arrived!" (Ok, some of us need a BIG cup of coffee to arrive, and many of us arrive a bit late each morning.) Anne Dillard makes a point by saying, "How we spend our days is how we spend our lives." How are you spending your days? Are they filled with things you love to do, with people you love to be with, and with work that you find fulfilling, satisfying, and meaningful? If not, spring is a most wonderful time to get up out of your rut and DO something about your life. Here are some tips for "Waking up."

1. **Get out**—out of your house, out of your office, and out of your mind. Get out into nature, do something physical, and move your body. Do something creative, unusual and the opposite of what you would "normally" do. GET RADICAL!

2. **Clean out**—spring-cleaning has not only a physical effect but an emotional effect as well. Uncluttering your home and office serves to create mental space to gain new perspectives and re-envision your goals. Take out all that old "garbage," figuratively and literally, to unburden yourself and make room for the new.

3. **Connect**—with friends, family, and people in your community. In the winter you tend to hibernate (as it should be per Mother Nature), so you may lose track of your relationships. Have you noticed that you haven't seen your neighbor all season? Write a note, send an e-mail, have a spring block party in your neighborhood to catch up.

4. **Handle Tolerations and Incompletions**. Tolerations are things that you put up with that drain your energy. Incompletions are things that hang over you left undone and drain you of mental energy. If you are putting up with something, such as gossip in the workplace, make a statement to eliminate this energy drain. Choose an alternative, positive channel for this energy. If you are worried that you haven't completed your taxes, file for an extension and make an appointment with yourself to sit down and complete the forms once and for all (at least for this year).

5. **Lighten Up**—take a day off to wallow in the sunshine. Go on a field trip with your kids. Invite your friends over for a potluck dinner. Go sailing or kayaking. Run a race for a favorite charity. Visit the circus. Do something FUN!

Nature calls us out to play in Springtime. Join her and renew your spirit!

Abundance

*I*t is far too easy to notice when you do not have something you want. Whether it is material goods or peace of mind, you always gravitate to that which you do not yet have.

Thanksgiving is typically the time for us to look with eyes wide open to that which you do have. How is it that people who must deal with disease or catastrophe may still be able to say thank you in the midst of their pain? For those who have been struck by illness or natural disaster or war, what lessons can they teach us regarding abundance?

There will always be pain, injustice and grief. But suffering is a choice much as joy is a choice. It is not only what occurs but also what meaning you attach to the events of your life. Noticing grief, pain and injustice allow you to meet this with the kind of "compassionate warriorship" that Pema Chodron, the Buddhist nun, speaks of in her books. A spiritual warrior does not run in the face of challenge but enters and learns, compassionately.

Where in your life are you feeling needy? Consider how this neediness may be sabotaging your efforts to move forward in your life. Is it silently driving you to be a certain way or do certain things that actually keep you from feeling successful or fulfilled? How might this neediness be filled in positive ways that come from a source of abundance instead of deprivation and scarcity?

If you are feeling the emptiness of a lost relationship, look to the relationships you enjoy and how you might spend more time cultivating those. In doing so, you may find this leads to new and energizing relationships.

If the financial crunch of the Holidays with its messages of materialism is affecting your mood, take another look at what you may have to contribute, from your heart, your talents, your hobbies, your time and elsewhere. These contributions are meaningful as they reflect your personal gifts to someone else.

As in all things, there is a harmony in your life that includes loss and gain, hardships and gifts. Seeking the abundance in your life will bring you more joy and create a resiliency that will assist you in dealing with whatever challenges you may face. Cultivate an attitude of abundance.

"And now here is my secret, a very simple secret:
It is only with the heart that one can see rightly;
what is essential is invisible to the eye."
The fox telling The Little Prince in The Little Prince:
~Antoine de Saint-Exupery

Thanks and Giving

What are you planning for Thanksgiving? Are you traveling? Will you be cooking for friends and family?

As Dorothy in "The Wizard of Oz" said, "There is no place like home." What does home mean for you? Is it a place, a structure, or a town? Is it the people around you? Is it the house where you grew up? Is it the house where you now live? What piece of the past have you carried into your present that feels like "home" to you? Moreover, why do you feel so welcomed when you return to our genuine home?

Returning home can be a way of connecting again to roots. The food you eat, the way it is cooked, the music that is played, and the generations of people who may gather give you a sense of both roots and familial evolution. It is a place you feel loved and welcomed. It is a place where you welcome the old, young and new. You gather to celebrate the connection and give thanks for all that means.

Not everyone defines home in the same way. For you, going back home, to your family or to the place where you grew up, brings up unresolved conflicts. Behind the festivities, there are shadows of past hurts. You may re-live the past as if it were here right now. Going home is not pleasant; it fills you with apprehension and worry.

Still for others, there is no home. There are shelters, churches and other organizations that will feed countless people, individuals who have encountered hardships in one form or another. As a friend of mine observed the other day,

"There by the grace of God go I."

Consider that home is also a place inside you. It is located in your heart and no matter where you are, you can choose to carry this home with you wherever you go. You can access this welcoming and secure place regardless of where you may be physically. If you are gathering in a joyous and loving place, open your internal home to the ones who celebrate with you. From this place, give thanks for having these people or places in your life.

If you are anticipating a holiday with conflict, try to stay centered in this internal home and from that safe place inside you, remain present to others without the need to change that which will not change. Perhaps in accepting what is there, and in being centered in your internal home, you may actually experience this holiday very differently. There is an opportunity here to observe with compassion and still honor your boundaries.

Remember that Thanksgiving is two words: thanks - for who and what we have in our lives; and giving - to those we know and love as well as to those who are connected to us on a more expansive level.

Wherever you go home to, I wish you abundance and many blessings each and every Thanksgiving.

Alicia Rodriguez

Reflections on a New Year

*E*ach New Year offers the chance to assess your past year and plan for the upcoming year. Here are some questions to ask yourself and some suggestions on how you can put your life into perspective in a way that frees you to begin each new year.

1. What did you accomplish in the past year? What helped you accomplish this?

2. What did you mean to accomplish in the past year but did not? What stood in your way?

3. How can you use these answers to move toward living a full life in the upcoming year?

4. What is left from the past year that is incomplete or unsaid? Complete it. Say it.

5. What do you have to be thankful for? Some things to be thankful for: people, relationships, a comfortable bed, food on the table. Give thanks, tell those you love that you love them, follow through with actions, and share your good fortune with others.

6. Even if you have encountered setbacks, what lies hidden in these events that gives you information on how next year could be better for you? What did you learn?

7. What, if anything, is the major change you need to make in order to realize a dream you have? How are you planning to make that change so your dream manifests?

8. Take some quiet time and define what is really important to you. Arrange your life accordingly.

9. What is in your life now that drains you of energy or holds you back? How much longer will you allow this to be present?

10. Choose one major direction or dream and on January 1 make a commitment - mind, body and soul - to that. You don't need to choose more than one but make it good!

*"What is Christmas? It is tenderness for the past,
courage for the present, hope for the future.
It is a fervent wish that every cup may overflow
with blessings rich and eternal,
and that every path may lead to peace."*
~ Agnes M. Pharo

Ho! Ho! Ho!

I still can't get over how quickly the Holidays come upon us! As I was finishing up last minute food shopping for Thanksgiving, I heard one of the first signs of the holidays – the Salvation Army bell ringer was standing outside the grocery store. Perhaps it's just me, but I still don't feel equipped to meet the Holidays so quickly.

I am not alone. Although this is a time that could be filled with laughter, joy and appreciation, for many it is a very stressful time. Mother Nature intended winter to be a time to look inward, yet everything in our culture is asking you to go OUT. Out shopping, out to parties, out visiting, out to finish whatever is unfinished in our year. No wonder you feel stressed; you are moving against "Nature's Tide".

Here are some tips to enjoy this time of celebration, regardless of your faith or religious affiliation, whether you celebrate Christmas, Hanukkah, Kwanzaa or any of the many other world holidays.

- **To give is as wonderful as to receive.** Giving does not have to be a material giving. You can give of your time, talents or presence. Some examples might be a coupon for babysitting, a freshly baked pie, or a handmade item. Children, in particular, can give something uniquely theirs.

- **Be at service.** This is a time when many who are not as fortunate may need a helping hand. Donate supplies to a school, take advantage of programs such as toys for tots, and help out at a fundraiser. Being at service is rewarding to the one at service as well as to the one being served.

• **Orient around what matter most to you.** Families, especially newly-weds or families with children, are pulled in numerous directions and are pressured to visit relatives or go to family events. Consider what the holidays mean to you. Where do you want to spend your Christmas morning? What are the rituals you want to have in your family? Perhaps you want to be in your own home on Christmas morning but will go visit others the next day? Orient around what really matters to you and your significant other, spouse and children and make decisions based on this.

• **Resist the pressure to be perfect.** Allow for some flexibility and spontaneity at this time. Your family dinner doesn't have to be perfect, instead, focus on enjoying the relationships instead of doing the dishes.

• **Remember those who will be missing.** Grief is particularly poignant at this time of year. If you or someone you know has lost someone in your life in this past year, be gentle with yourself or with that person. The holidays can be particularly difficult if you are dealing with loss as well.

• **Focus on the true meaning of the holidays.** And I am not talking about Wal-Mart's message. What does this time mean to you spiritually. Reconnect with that.

• **Give yourself plenty of time.** Don't over-commit

yourself. Make time for yourself and those that really matter to you first. The rest is optional.

• **Be a kid again.** I love watching my son when we visit Lights on the Bay in Annapolis. He is full of awe and wonder and I am only too happy to join him in this. At Sandy Point Park in Annapolis, a drive - through scenario with lights depicting holiday scenes is one of our most enjoyable things to do during the holidays. And as a fund-raiser, it feels good donating the entrance fee to a good cause.

• **Appreciate all the good things.** Be sure to take time to appreciate the good in your life and to share this with others.

Don't overdo it. Eat well and in a healthy way, get plenty of sleep and if you have time off, extra cuddling is especially nice on wintry mornings!

Journaling Notes

Use this area to write down your insights and epiphanies that you want to remember. Maybe they are random thoughts, a drawing, a dream or a declaration about something you want. Putting it into writing brings it to life and attracts possibilities.

Acknowledgments

I have been writing *EveryDay Epiphanies* for years as an online newsletter. Countless clients and friends, inspiring me to think deeper about what seems obvious and to probe into what is hidden, have fueled my thoughts and insights.

As a coach, I have been witness to so many of my client's epiphanies. When asked why I do this work I answer, "I do it for the 'AHA' moment." That is the moment where a light shines in a person's eyes, their breath becomes still and something at their core shifts and expands, never to return to the same place again. It doesn't matter who it is, what their title is, what they do for a living or anything else. What matters is that my clients have undertaken a courageous journey, a soul-centered journey, into their hearts and minds and in taking the step, they open the door to countless possibilities.

I am privileged to walk this road with many individuals. For me, what really matters is that I make a difference using whatever gifts I have. So indeed, being in the presence of the inquiry and courage that happens in coaching returns the gift.

I tell people that everyone should have a personal theme song and a personal mantra that may change as their lives change. One of my theme songs has been the Beatles, "I get by with a little help from my friends." And so, I must acknowledge my friends who have "walked through the fire" with me, or I with them, on many occasions. Had it not been for these experiences I might've always remained "in the muck".

I want to acknowledge someone whom I have never met in person but over time we have created a sisterly bond that has contributed greatly to this book and to my life. She lives in the northern parts of Maine, a state close to my heart, and while I enjoy tulips in March, she is usually still digging out of snowfalls. Sandy Gibson, my webmaster, publisher of my online newsletter and dear friend, pushed me to make this book happen. If it were not for her, I feel that I would never have enjoyed the success in my businesses or in my life as truly they are woven together. Thank you Sandy.

I would like to thank Blooming Twig Books LLC and Kent Gustavson PhD, a musician and writer himself, who believes in authors and their works. He challenged me to improve my writing and encouraged me to publish this book. Although I met him only recently I have come to admire his commitment to writers and to all creative artists and I appreciate his generous spirit.

One essay in this book is dedicated to my mother, Mina Rodriguez. There is no way I can thank her enough. Her quirky sayings (in Spanish) and her advice have helped me forge a life based in choice and self-accountability. Together with my father who died in 1976, she has demonstrated true courage and optimism. Both parents believed in me and because of them, I believe in myself and in my ability to create what I want and need in life, oftentimes despite evidence to the contrary. In Mina's declining years, it has been difficult for her and for me but I now know that this special connection between us will always exist regardless of distance, regardless of any obstacles between us and regardless of her presence on this earth.

To my husband, Gerard Connolly, I can say, what a journey! Through good times and not so good times we have stood side by side and we have learned the meaning of true commitment and friendship. He has always encouraged me to explore my personal and spiritual development, much of which forms the foundation of my writing.

A special thank you to the Gameboy Guru whose entry into my life woke me up. I was already on the path but nothing like a child to teach you presence and attention!

I love you Joseph.

And a last thank you to you, my readers. So many of you wrote responses to my online essays that it was inevitable that I would notice the impact of my writing. We are all connected in our mutual human experience and EveryDay Epiphanies is an expression of that connection. You inspire me to keep writing!

I am sure there are others I need to thank and I apologize that I cannot mention each person so to all of you, thank you for your support, your encouragement and for sharing your thoughts and epiphanies with me. Your "AHA" moments mean the world to me.

In gratitude,

Alicia Rodriguez
Annapolis, MD
September 9, 2007

About the Author

*F*ormerly from the Boston area, Alicia Rodriguez now resides near Annapolis, MD with her husband, Gerard, her son Joseph (aka Gameboy Guru) and her four-footed son, Bailey-dog. She writes from her extensive experience coaching individuals from all walks of life.

Her intense curiosity about the nature of what it means to be human fuels her candid observations and contributes to her success as a "wisdom partner" to her clients.

Through her firm, Sophia Associates, Inc., Alicia works with leaders, high potential executives and successful entrepreneurs and professionals who value her keen intuition and her role as a challenging yet empathetic sounding board. She writes freelance for numerous online and paper magazines and is a sought-after speaker and seminar leader on issues of leadership, gender in organizations, diversity and creativity. She is also a passionate advocate for women in organizations and for women's organizations against domestic violence.

In her free time she enjoys chilled wine with good friends, poetry, long walks in Nature, profound conversations over good food, summertime sitting on "her rock" on an island in Maine and remembering how to play like a kid with her son and dog.

For information on coaching services,
speaking engagements, seminars and more,
visit *Sophia Associates, Inc.* on the web
at www.sophia-associates.com

For personal coaching
visit *Soul Centered Life Management*
on the web at www.sclmcoach.com

For more information on EveryDay Epiphanies, and
to order the book EveryDay Epiphanies online,
visit www.everyday-epiphanies.com